THE TRIUMPH OF

CLASSICAL MANAGEMENT

OVER

LEAN MANAGEMENT

How Tradition Prevails
And What To Do About It

BOB EMILIANI, PH.D.

The Triumph of Classical Management Over Lean Management: How Tradition Prevails and What to Do About It / Bob Emiliani

Cover design by Bob Emiliani
Cover photos courtesy of Peace Dale Library, Jessica Wilson. Peace Dale Manufacturing Company, Peace Dale, Rhode Island, ca. 1900. Used with permission.
Interior font: Garamond

ISBN-13: 978-0-9898631-9-3
Library of Congress Control Number: 2018901461

1. Leadership 2. Economics 3. Political Science 4. Business 5. Management 6. Lean

First Edition: February 2018 • Updated December 2018

Published by Cubic LLC, South Kingstown, Rhode Island, USA

CONTENTS

This book is dedicated to those who
failed to engage their leaders in Lean
management. Now you know why.

Preface

I first encountered the Toyota production system (TPS) while I was a business unit manager in one of Pratt & Whitney's manufacturing facilities, courtesy of Shingijutsu consultants. TPS came to me relatively late in my industry career. Nevertheless, my introduction to it was an eye-opening experience – as it is to many people. Yet, even at the start, it was clear that some of my peer managers were more excited about TPS than others. At the executive level, interest TPS was uneven, and hands-on engagement in learning TPS was not among executives' interests.

The unusual reactions to TPS among business leaders troubled me. I could not understand why something so practical and promising did not instantly attract every manager to learn TPS and lead its practice throughout the company. After all, it has the potential to relieve many of management's repetitive burdens and make the job of leadership easier, more effective, and far more fulfilling.

Over time, I came to realize that what I had observed and experienced was not unusual. In fact, it was the common condition. Executives and managers showed little interest in TPS, while many of those who did were actually faking it. I wanted to know why. Starting in 1996, I began an extended study of TPS and its derivative, Lean, informed by my daily practice and research studies. I wrote dozens of academic papers and 18 books. This was among my most rewarding professional experiences. But, despite all the writing and all the progress I had made in understanding why executives and managers were disinterested in TPS and Lean, I felt that I was not yet done. I had not answered the questions to my satisfaction. So, I pressed forward, and this book is the result of my most recent efforts. It is the culmination of 20 years of work.

The focus of this book is Lean in its current formulation as a management system – Lean management system (LMS) – derived from Toyota's management system (TMS). Additionally, the focus of this book is large corporations, and why executives therein typically show disinterest in Lean (and TMS as well). However, the findings also apply to executives in small- and mid-size corporations, as well as government and non-profit organizations.

Executive disinterest in progressive management is actually a 100-year-old problem, dating back to the start of Scientific Management (ca. 1890-1940). The creators of Scientific Management also found widespread disinterest in their new system of management, especially among the leaders of large corporations. The problem has persisted over a long stretch of time, and thus has never been clearly understood, let alone solved, until now.

You may ask, "Why bother solving this problem?" There are numerous reasons:

- Curiosity about the problem
- The challenge of solving a complex problem that has existed for a long time
- To better understand executive thinking
- Advance the understanding of TMS and LMS

- Establish work that others can build upon (e.g. the neurological basis for what is expressed in this book)
- To identify practical solutions
- Help people who have struggled to advance Lean in their organizations

I remained committed to solving this problem for more than 20 years because it can help people now and in the future — for the everyday problems they face, or perhaps even for averting crises or dealing with crises.

The findings are not what the proponents of Lean management want to hear. They might not like what they read and feel somewhat defeated. But they should not feel that way. Problems that are solved create new knowledge which should result in these outcomes:

1. Expose new problems that need to be solve
2. Generate ideas to further advance knowledge, in search of more successful outcomes
3. Modify the current methods for Lean training and Lean transformation
4. Abandon Lean management and move on to another subject or activity of interest

People fully committed to Lean will chose first, second, and third outcomes. Some will choose the fourth outcome, which is certainly acceptable. This book provides a basis for choosing any of the four outcomes.

After reading this book, you may not comprehend an immediate practical benefit. Don't worry about that. There are many lines of research that do not have immediate practical benefit, such as classification of insect species or solving theoretical mathematical problems (such as Fermat's Last Theorem). But, what it does is develop new insights and new problem-solving methods.

The existing understanding of TMS and LMS, and Scientific Management before that, was not capable of solving the problem of executive disinterest. So, I set out to create a new understanding of the problem and develop new practical insights. To do this, I used a combination of historical, ethnographic, descriptive, and causal research methods. In addition, I make use of my two decades worth of experience with TMS and LMS in my capacities as a practitioner, educator, and executive trainer.

Based on work that I had done in prior years, I knew the true source of the problem was related to two branches of the social sciences: economics and political science. Instead of relying on contemporary works, I went back in time and read numerous social science books and papers from the late 19th and early 20th century to look for clues. I wanted to understand the thinking of a century or more ago that informed contemporary executive thinking and action.

Going back in time proved to be a fruitful activity that filled in numerous details and answered many of questions. The result was a series of four research papers that accomplish the following:

- Revealed fundamental errors in understanding made from the start of Lean (and Scientific Management before that)
- Significantly advanced the understanding of why efforts to transform large organizations (and medium and small ones as well) fall short or fail completely — since the inception of progressive management over 100 years ago
- Identified potential solutions for people to experiment with

The research papers were originally posted on my blog in late 2017 and 2018. I received extraordinary praise for the papers, summarized by this typical comment: "Your insights get to the heart of the matter and ring true" and "Brilliant and gives hope for the future." I have collected the four papers in this volume to provide readers with a convenient single source for the work, with added context to help people understand how it came about, what it means, how it can help them in their work to advance TMS or LMS, and also provide an alternative improvement pathway for those who are interested in trying something new.

It is my hope that you find this volume to be interesting, useful, and inspiring. I challenge readers to build on this work, as well as my entire body of work, to advance the knowledge, understanding, and practice of TMS and LMS so that business and society can move forward.

Bob Emiliani
South Kingstown, Rhode Island
February 2018

Introduction

We hold business and business leaders in high regard. There are many sound reasons for this, as business does much good for society. Yet, to an extent much greater than we realize, businesspersons are receivers of settled wisdom which they readily accept and transmit to others. Over time, there is a concatenation of transmitters and receivers, more-or-less uncritical at any step, unable to gain emancipation from preconceptions that inhibit needed evolution in business thinking and management practice. And, the general tendency is to interpret things along the way with ever-greater departure from fact and the well-being of individuals and society. As a result, discord is generated between business and society, to the benefit of neither.

The inability to abandon preconceptions arises from executive disinterest in the methods of production, whether goods or services. A simpler way of stating this is that executives do not have interest in how workers perform their work. Work processes, being of no interest, are delegated to other people – the workers themselves, or technical specialists in processes and process improvement. The point of executive interest is the result obtained by the process. That, in turn, is related to the line of interest that that fully absorbs executive attention: business dealings and financial results.

The ends being of greater interest than the means has the effect of adulterating management practice such that management practice evolves towards that which requires the least effort and which yields the most gain. Management is rife with shortcuts and substitutions to achieve the required business result. And, nominally, these shortcuts and substitutions do achieve the required result, though, unfortunately, some may suffer. What a business leader says is necessary today – based on rock-solid belief – is often abandoned tomorrow in favor of a new shortcut or substitution. Observers call the leader a hypocrite, but from the leader's perspective it is nothing more than a necessary change made with a wholly good and ethical conscience. The change is nearly always defensible from the perspectives that matter most: business, legal, and political (and captured in the dictum "what is good for business is good for society"). As a result, efforts to repair, reform, or transform management face a nearly insurmountable challenge.

This is the challenge that Lean faced when it first came into public attention in 1988. In hindsight, it seems clear that the magnitude of the challenge was misunderstood, and therefore, the methods used for decades to gain executive's interest in Lean were unsuitable. More than ever before, the research presented in this book clearly illuminates the misunderstanding and the magnitude of the challenge. It also offers several potential solutions for those who wish to carry forward efforts to advance Lean management and gain wider acceptance for it in corporations of all types and sizes.

A summary of the research findings can be simply stated as follows: Lean must be led by an organization's top leaders because it requires changes in strategies, policies and practices that only top executives can make. However, the research shows the existence of numerous social and economic rules that disallow leaders from learning and leading Lean. This results in a contradiction whose resolution is impossible under typical conditions (Chapter 1) – but which can advance to improbable under atypical conditions (Chapters 2 and 3). And, resolution may ultimately have to be forced upon leaders (Chapter 4).

It is almost a Catch-22 type of problem, where the solution is nearly impossible due to the existence of contradictory rules:

- Leaders are needed to learn Lean and lead Lean transformation
- Leaders are not allowed to learn or lead Lean due to various social and economic rules
- Therefore, leaders don't learn or lead Lean

This, of course, is not true in every case. What we find is great disinterest in Lean management, in its full form, by executives in large corporations. Success with Lean has been more common with mid-size and small companies. However, when one realizes the huge number of mid-size and small businesses in existence, the uptake of Lean management is miniscule. That suggests there is something fundamentally wrong with Lean management, that executives have different mindsets and better methods for achieving their objectives, or both. Mindsets and methods that yield the greatest gain with the least amount of effort are formidable competitors to Lean management. In fact, such mindsets and methods, if unchanged, condemn Lean rather than make it an item of executive interest.

It is of no consequence if most, or all, of the executive mindset is rooted in ancient, theoretical, spiritual, or divine preconceptions related to business. The fact is, executives have mental and physical processes that, to their understanding, work perfectly fine and fully satisfy their business and personal needs. Yet, these clearly result in deficits in executive functioning and business performance, but they are not recognized as a problem with wide-ranging impact.

This book puts a spotlight on various specific features of executive culture, economics, and politics (social influence within and external to a company) that allow readers to easily comprehend, in great detail, that which previously was understood in only hazy outlines. From this new knowledge, more effective strategies can be devised, and actions taken to advance Lean management.

It seems the problem that has plagued progressive management since its inception over 100 years ago has now been either been fully solved or is very close to finally being solved. However, no matter how complete a solution may be, there are unsolved elements or details of the problem that lurk in the background and will unexpectedly come to the forefront. As a result, problem recognition and problem-solving must be ongoing. In addition, circumstances change with time, requiring modification of the understanding of the problem, and the solutions to be adjusted or the creation of new solutions.

This research has received extraordinary praise from people in the Lean community who have toiled for years to gain executive acceptance for Lean management in their company or organization. They see it as an accurate reflection of conditions that they experienced first-hand, often over a period of decades. So, the research rings true. Yet, extraordinary praise and truth means little if people are unable, for whatever reasons, to turn what they learned into practical strategies and tactics for change.

Several people have noted that the research papers reproduced in Chapters 1, 2, and 3 explain more than the case of why Lean management has struggled to gain acceptance. They see the research has solving the general case of why company-wide management improvement efforts, such as TQM, Six Sigma, Lean Six Sigma, Agile, and Kata also struggle to gain acceptance among executive and often fail. Therefore, this book provides important insights that can be useful for many different types of corporate transformation efforts.

As should be obvious, business school education of current and future leaders remains weak by the standards of progressive management practice such as that embodied by Toyota's management system. While education in the mechanics of quantitative analysis is strong, this capability cannot stand apart from qualitative analytical capabilities. The two must be used in combination. The current approach to business school education – strong in quantitative analytics and weak in qualitative analytics (critical thinking and the scientific method) – means that graduates of both degree programs and executive education programs will carry forth as their predecessors did in the past. In other words, no substantive change to management and leadership practice, despite the great need for evolution.

This book can help fill the gap by teaching current and future leaders how to break free from the past so that business and society can evolve and improve. But, why is it important for leadership and management to evolve and improve when business looks to be in good shape? Why change, especially given that the current state is so effective at preserving vested rights and vested interests?

There are two facts that nobody can deny: times change and needs change. While the needs of business can be forced by executives to remain the same, the needs of society evolve. Business is an important and far-reaching contributor to society, and management practice (inclusive of leadership) is its animating method of control. Highly compensated executives are not employed for the purpose of managing a business in ways that result in consistently performing at levels below that which can be reasonably attained. When management practice fails to evolve, business suffers and so does society.

Executives are entrusted with the responsibility to guide the company as times change and assure its continued existence through continuous upgrades to competitiveness. And competitive strength is defined first and foremost by how leadership and management are practiced, as this determines the level of engagement of employees (and suppliers). The management method used regulates the ability of business leaders to execute their fiduciary and non-fiduciary responsibilities – as well as the level of capability among employees to effectively execute plans in a timely manner. It would seem a wise choice to use a management method that enables, rather than handicaps, corporate performance.

In professional sports, athletes seek even the tiniest competitive advantage. Yet, in business, professional leaders ignore huge opportunities for competitive advantage. Leaders can make that choice simply because they are the ones in charge. But, just because one can do something does not mean it is a wise or appropriate thing to do.

This book concretely shows how unwise and inappropriate methods of leadership and management come into being and remain in force over generations of leaders. If there is one overarching learning from this book, it is that the most basic demands progressive management places on leaders are a severe infringement upon their vested rights and interests. But, it also shows how change can be made so that management practice will evolve continuously, for the benefit of both business and society.

I am under no illusion that many people invested in Lean will not appreciate my research or be open-minded to it. They may interpret it negatively because of its impact on their work, their influence, or their business. My hope is that they interpret this book as an effort to help them to understand the current state so that they work towards a more successful future state.

Ultimately, I would like this work to be seen as useful research that has unraveled longstanding mysteries, and which inspires people to improve their practice of leadership and management.

1

A Study of Executive Resistance to Lean

Abstract

As we approach the 30th anniversary of Lean, we see that Lean is both everywhere and nowhere. It is seemingly everywhere in terms of its tools and methods, but virtually nowhere in terms of its use as a comprehensive system of management in large corporations. The question is why, despite decades of effort? While myriad explanations have been offered, none have considered the role of executive culture in any detail. This chapter seeks to correct that by examining executive culture and showing how numerous elements of executive culture combine to create a nearly impenetrable bulwark against the intrusion of Lean as a replacement for classical management practice. While the findings offer no easy solution to this difficult problem, they illustrate the perils of assuming one knows an audience and how best to influence that audience. Specifically, by using various logical and rational means to persuade a prominent class of wealthy and influential people whose interests are far more complex, nuanced, and interdependent than is immediately visible or which they are willing to voluntarily reveal or perhaps even realize. Exposing the complexity and interdependent features of executive culture illuminates the challenge ahead for those who still hope to gain widespread acceptance of Lean management by the corporate executive class.

Note: This chapter explores the research question: Why do executives resist Lean management?

Introduction

Thirty years ago, John Krafcik (Krafcik, 1988) brought the words "Lean production" into public awareness as a generic term to describe Toyota's production system (TPS). Soon thereafter, James P. Womack and Daniel T. Jones assumed the role of Lean movement leaders (Womack and Jones, 1990, 1996) and served as its leading advocates and promoters through today. From the start, there were substantial differences between TPS (Monden, 1983; Ohno, 1988) and Lean. Over time, these two production methods further diverged from one another, as shown in Figure 1-1, in an apparent effort to make Lean more attractive to the top executives of large corporations. This effort continues today and now includes a closer alignment to TPS and the claim that Lean is a corporate strategy (Byrne, 2012; Ballé et al., 2017).

Despite a persistent and gallant effort over three decades, Womack and Jones have been unsuccessful in gaining interest in Lean among the chief executive officers of large corporations. CEOs, as a group, have been particularly resistant to Lean as a management system and the process necessary to transform a business from classical (viz., antiquated, archaic) management and leadership practice to modern Lean management and leadership practice. The precise reasons for executive resistance to Lean have long been poorly understood. They are typically attributed to diffuse personality traits such as "command-and-control" (Byrne, 2012), hubris, impatience, closed-mindedness, or other characteristics such as an inability to change or intolerance to criticism. Not understanding the precise

Method	Toyota Production System (1947→)	Lean Production (1988-1995)	Lean Production (1996-2006)	Lean Management (2007-2016)	Lean Strategy (2017→)
Designer	Industrial Engineers[1]	Mechanical Engineer[2]	Social Scientists[3]	Social Scientists[3]	Businessperson[4]
Goal	Cost Reduction Productivity Improvement	Quality Productivity	Customer Value	Maximize Customer Value	Deliver More Value to Customers
Principles	Continuous Improvement Respect for People	Continuous Improvement	Specify Value Identify the Value Stream Flow Pull Perfection	Purpose Process People	Improve Customer Satisfaction Improve the Flow of Work Make it Easier to Get Tasks Done Right the First Time Improve Relationships
Normal Condition	Flow	Flow	Perfect Processes	Perfect Processes	Think Differently
Focus of Improvement	Human	Technical	Technical	Technical / Human	Human
Primary Teaching Method	Gemba Kaizen	Team Leader	Classroom	Classroom / Gemba	Gemba Kaizen
Object of Interest	Waste, Unevenness, Unreasonableness	Inventories	Value Creating Activities	Value Creating Activities	Learning
Desired Outcome	Customer Satisfaction Survival	High Plant Performance	Wealth Creation	Perfect Value	Winning

Figure 1-1. Some of the primary differences between the Toyota Production System and its derivative, Lean, as Lean has evolved since its inception in 1988.

1 Taiichi Ohno, *Toyota Production System* (1988), *Workplace Management* (1988), *Just-in-Time for Today and Tomorrow* (1988), and Ohno's team. 2 John Krafcik, "Triumph of the Lean Production System" (*Sloan Management Review*, Fall 1988) https://www.lean.org/downloads/MITSloan.pdf. 3 James P. Womack and Daniel T. Jones, *Lean Thinking* (1996) and http://www.lean.org/WhatsLean/ (accessed 22 August 2017); 4 Art Byrne by way of M. Ballé et al., *Lean Strategy* (2017), https://www.lean.org/LeanPost/Posting.cfm?LeanPostId=770, and http://theleanstrategy.com/

sources of resistance are a fundamental barrier to the advancement of Lean management and to broaden its base of adoption across all industries.

In a recent article, James P. Womack recounted the struggles that he experienced and admits that Lean has proven to be unacceptable to the leaders of large corporations (Womack, 2017):

> **"With regards to denial, we need to acknowledge that our efforts to dramatically transform large, mature organizations haven't worked and aren't going to work, even when these organizations encounter crises.** I spent several years recently with CEOs of large enterprises and got them to sanction model lines for value streams to demonstrate what was possible. The results were strikingly positive, but the organizational immune reaction was immediate and crushing. Little lasting was achieved and I've moved on. I no longer expect 'another Toyota' to emerge in every mature industry." (Bold in original)

This recognition is not unique to Womack and Jones. The few CEOs who led what are widely considered to be successful Lean transformation processes, most notably Arthur Byrne (Byrne, 2012), in addition to a small group of other CEOs, readily admit that they too have had little success in influencing their peer CEOs. Whether one is a movement leader or a successful CEO, the outcome remains the same: Little appetite for Lean among the leaders of large corporations despite decades of effort. As will be shown later, Lean CEOs are seen by their peers as deviants or abnormalities in an otherwise uniform and well-behaved executive class in command of the classical means and mechanisms used to achieve favorable business results.

More generally, it is widely acknowledged within the Lean community that there has been far less recognition and acceptance of Lean as a more effective system of management than was originally imagined. CEOs have proven themselves to be highly resistant to Lean management. The question is why? Why have four or five generations of CEOs across every industry sector largely dismissed Lean in favor of maintaining classical management practices? Why has the evidence of better management practice and superior business results been ignored? And why have shareholders and other stakeholders accepted management's decision to forego Lean?

Over the years, there has been much speculation as to the causes of the observed effect – which, simply put, is the "failure to establish Lean as a management system in large corporations" (see Appendix for a formal failure analysis). This includes factors such as:

- The failure of business schools to teach Lean
- Poor quality Lean training courses, programs, and workshops
- Consultants who are unqualified to teach Lean
- Confusion about what Lean is and is not
- Variations and derivatives of Lean

- Changing definitions of Lean
- No discernable business results from Lean practice
- Slow accumulation of business results
- Absence of executive engagement in Lean
- Absence of executive support for Lean
- Absence of leadership by executives

There is no doubt that these and other causes have had a deleterious effect on the acceptance of Lean among top executives. Being a difficult, interconnected problem, with abundant reinforcing and restraining loops, there are numerous causes that contribute to the observed effect. When faced with such a problem, there is a tendency to ignore simple answers in favor of more complex ones. But, is there one simple cause that influences many, even perhaps most, of the other easily identifiable causes? In other words, is there a cause, hiding in plain sight, that influences most of the other causes? If a such a cause exists, will understanding it help Lean advocates devise new strategies and tactics to gain acceptance for Lean among CEOs and establish Lean as the dominant system of management practice in large corporations in the future?

The promotion of Lean moved forward three decades ago under numerous bedrock assumptions that were untested and therefore taken to be true, and which, in turn, makes the adoption of Lean by executives seem to be a *fait accompli*. The bedrock assumptions include:

- People want to learn and improve
- People are not afraid of change

- Managers like to experiment and try new things
- Managers are willing to change
- Managers are willing to think differently
- Managers are willing to lead major change
- Managers are receptive to a better system of management
- Managers can be persuaded by rational/logical arguments
- Being shown better ways will be enthusiastically accepted
- Personal success/pride will be subjugated to pursue new opportunities
- Workers don't like to be told what to do
- Workers want to be free to think, create, and innovate
- Teamwork is more desirable than individualism
- Organizational hierarchies pose no limitations/barriers
- Strong organizations want to become stronger
- Weak organizations want to become stronger with Lean
- The executive culture is understood

Assumptions taken to be true blind people to other possible causal relationships. Incorrect assumptions lead to mistakes due to an inability to see what is in plain sight. The present study is focused on the last assumption listed, that the executive culture was understood by Womack, Jones, as well as most others, at the start in 1988 and remained understood for three decades thereafter. In retrospect, it seems clear that this assumption was incorrect, especially given that business leaders in the Progressive Era also shunned the then-form of progressive management known as "Scientific management" (Taylor, 1911), as exemplified by these words written by one of Taylor's close associates (Person, 1947):

> "In the course of his [1912] testimony before the House committee [to Investigate the Taylor and Other Systems of Shop Management], Taylor was asked how many concerns used his system in its entirety. His reply was: 'In its entirety – none; not one.' Then, in response to another question he went on to say that a great many used it substantially, to a greater or less degree. Were Mr. Taylor alive to respond to the same question in 1947 – thirty-five years later – his reply would have to be essentially the same."

By the early 1930s, the leaders of Scientific management were consonant in their discouragement. They could not understand why CEOs of large companies ignored the evidence of better management practice and superior business performance that they discovered and developed over time. Some 90 years ago, they gave up their quest for the answer and declared that psychology and the emerging field of leadership studies would one day provide the answer. Since then, these fields of study blossomed and produced mountains of useful information, but no answer to the basic question: Why do generations of CEOs across every industry sector strenuously maintain classical management practices and, by extension, shun new systems of progressive management with such great vigor?

The answer to this question is of great practical importance because of its relationship to economic system strength, the business cycle, societal wealth (especially middle-class wealth) and well-being, resource consumption, international competitiveness, and national security. Few questions have an answer as consequential as this.

This study seeks to understand the present problem, executive resistance to Lean, through the lens of past studies of socioeconomic phenomena. In particular, wealth and the culture and characteristics of the people who possess it (Veblen, 1899). This Veblenesque socioeconomic interpretation (see Note 1) offers a plausible and detailed understanding of the culture and causal relationships that delineate executive resistance to Lean. This perspective will be useful to others in their efforts to promote Lean management or a future version of progressive management that may one day replace Lean.

Finally, readers should carefully note the aim of this chapter, which is nothing more than a narrow interest to dispassionately discover, understand, and describe a curious phenomenon in business as it relates to wealth, economics, labor, and human relations. In that process, executive culture reveals itself to be a formidable and complex combination of interwoven characteristics that cannot be easily disentangled, thus making it difficult for Lean to gain entry and acceptance.

Division of Labor

Division of labor creates division of occupation. Occupation is a useful proxy for class, given that large numbers of occupations can be grouped into a few discrete social classes. The classes, in turn, embody differences in culture. What is culture? Schein (1996) defined culture as:

> "A culture is a set of basic tacit assumptions about how the world is and ought to be that a group of people share and that determines their perceptions, thoughts, feelings, and, to some degree, their overt behavior. Culture manifests itself at three levels: the level of deep tacit assumptions that are the essence of the culture, the level of espoused values that often reflect what a group wishes ideally to be and the way it wants to present itself publicly, and the day-to-day behavior that represents a complex compromise among the espoused values, the deeper assumptions, and the immediate requirements of the situation."

Importantly, culture may not be precisely what it seems, and therefore must be carefully deconstructed and decoded (Schein, 1996):

> "Overt behavior alone cannot be used to decipher culture because situational contingencies often make us behave in a manner that is inconsistent with our deeper values and assumptions. For this reason, one often sees 'inconsistencies' or 'conflicts' in overt behavior or between behavior and

espoused values. To discover the basic elements of a culture, one must either observe behavior for a very long time or get directly at the underlying values and assumptions that drive the perceptions and thoughts of the group members."

Hence, what one might logically or rationally expect from a set of behaviors is often contradicted. This is especially true where one has the means to sustain "inconsistencies or conflicts" with few or no consequences to one's self. In other words, wealthy business persons suffer little from "inconsistencies or conflicts" (Parker and Rucker, 2017), while manual laborers suffer greatly, as it typically results in employment setbacks, wage setbacks, or job loss.

Within each different type of divided labor lies a different culture. The workers who tan leather hides have a different culture than the workers who make shoes. People who work in finance have a different culture than those who work in accounting. The same is true for mechanical and civil or electrical engineers. And, as people change positions or rise with a hierarchy, they assume the culture of the occupation. For example, a laborer who becomes an engineer, then a manager, and then an executive will adopt the culture at each level to be effective in the job and to survive.

Inhomogeneities in culture can be small but still significant, such as between corporate and public accounting. Culture can also be largely homogeneous, as in the case of hierarchies wherein subordinates are in direct and frequent contact with their leader, such as a president and their vice presidents, each of whom represents a different functional area with its own unique sub-culture. This accounts for the common difficulty that executives experience when seeking to align an organization to a unified direction as defined by strategy, goals, and objectives.

What is the executive culture and what is the evidence that describes it? Executive culture can be characterized by evidence of its preoccupations and evidence of class distinctions. First is the evidence of its preoccupations using Veblen's taxonomy (Veblen, 1899), which recalls the interests of tribal chieftains or monarchs, transposed into the affairs of business and business persons (see Note 2). They are:

War

- Competition in the marketplace
- Control of the marketplace
- Conflict between management and labor
- Conflict between company and suppliers

Hunting

- Mergers and acquisitions
- Hostile takeovers
- Seizure of assets
- New customers

Sports

- Negotiations (duels)
- Mock and ridicule others
- Boast of one's prowess
- Political attacks on rivals

Devout Observances
- Etiquette and decorum
- Executive offsite meetings
- Earnings reports and conference calls
- Shareholder meetings
- Scapegoat (sacrifice)

Executive preoccupation is with matters related to property and property rights (ownership): fighting, displays of strength and prowess, seizure, and conquest. For any win there must be a loser. Unambiguous zero-sum outcomes are required to clearly signal the superior class and the inferior class, and to serve notice of the expected outcome should future conflicts arise. Executive preoccupation is also with matters related to personal relationships between subordinates, peers, and superiors. These four preoccupations are the viewpoint from which facts and events in business are comprehended and acted upon. Importantly, they form the basis for defining one's honor and the conduct of acts which are perceived as honorific by the executive class.

Next comes the evidence of class distinctions. Such distinctions are apparent to anyone who has worked in a corporation, especially those who have successfully advanced in the hierarchy. These include:

Superior Status:
- Physical separation from workers
- Limited contact with workers
- Rank and grade level

- Reviews and approvals (gatekeeper role)
- Remuneration
- Style of dress (uniform)
- Corporate perks (dining, travel)
- Exclusive business gatherings
- Exclusive social gatherings

Wealth:
- Remuneration
- Style of dress (uniform)
- Adornments (watches and jewelry)
- Automobile, home, and hobbies
- Patron of luxury goods and services

Invidiousness:
- Organizational politics
- Size of department, budget, etc.
- Gossip and innuendo
- Humiliation and put-downs
- "Shoot the messenger"

Non-Productive Consumption of Time:
- Meetings
- Indecision
- Delays
- Bureaucracy
- Conservatism (status quo)
- Corporate-speak (speak but not say anything, produce "noble gases")

- Organizational politics

These provide a general outline of the executive culture. It forms a habit of mind, one of predation and hostility towards others, which perpetually reinforces classifications of people and the type of work that they do, such that status is clearly separable and easily identifiable, and to thwart others who seek to gain at the expense of the executive class. Any loss by the executive class is perceived, most importantly, as a loss of honor, followed by a loss of wealth and a loss of power and influence.

It is notable that this culture survives from ancient times, not by chance, but by intention. Preservation of the executive culture is an honorific act that members of the class seek to perpetuate. Progressive management in general, and Lean in particular, is pernicious and has the power to rapidly undermine the executive culture. It requires intolerable losses of honor and diminution of wealth, property, power, and influence. In the limit, Lean is perceived as having the ability to render many major elements of executive class culture obsolete (Table 1-1). As a result, executives allow only certain minor elements of Lean to be adopted – those related to aesthetics and thrift – to appear current and in good fashion, while fully avoiding any harm to their valuable executive culture. Should any peril arise, the minor elements of Lean will be quickly subsumed into a bureaucracy controllable by the executives – though often at significant expense. One can easily imagine modest executive distemper towards Womack and Jones for having created Lean, which was far more difficult for them to ignore than Toyota's production method.

Table 1-1: Some Differences in Executive Culture

Attribute	Classical	Lean
Dominant Cultural Characteristic	War, Fighting	Peace, Communication
Relationship	Predatory, Opportunistic, Promiscuous	Symbiotic, Humanitarian, Faithful
Business Design	Feudal	Co-Op
Governing Authority	Invisible Hand	Self-Help
Key Leader Characteristic	Hubris	Humility
Relationships	Value Defined by Class	Value Defined by Need
Hierarchical Affection	High	Low
Dominant Concern	Investors	Customers
Decision-Making Inputs	Few	Many
Level of Commitment	Transient (dating)	Long-Term (marriage)
Honorific Outcome	Winning	Mutual Prosperity
Control Ethos	Regulate, Stagnate	Innovate, Evolve
Level of Involvement	Low, Detached	High, Engaged
Character Trait	Greed	Sharing
Remuneration	Lavish	Balanced
Point of View	Served by Others	Service to Others
Respect	Abuse Others	Help Others
Beauty	Expensive, Complex	Low Cost, Simple
Work (labor)	Taboo	Get Hands Dirty
Problem-Solving	Ad Hoc	Structured
Value of Etiquette	High	Low
Value of Privilege	High	Low

Table 1-1: Some Differences in Executive Culture (Con't)

Attribute	Classical	Lean
Personal Success Recognition	Conspicuous, Loud	Enigmatic, Quiet
Point of Equilibrium	Year-Over-Year Increase in Growth and Profits	Continuous Improvement and Respect for People
Unit of Performance	Individual	Team
Formal Education	End of Learning	Beginning of Learning
Value of Human	High for Executives (peers)	High for Workers
Economic Basis for Business	Classical Political Economy	German Historical School

Property, Wealth, and Honor

What is it that helps the executive culture survive and prosper? Is it limited to the four preoccupations and actuating class differences in day-today business activities? Or, do they use leverage to maintain and expand their class and their culture? If so, what is that leverage? The leverage is classical political economy.

Historically, business owners as a class are wealthy, while the agents (managers) that owners hired to administrate the business day-to-day were far less wealthy. That is until the late 1970s, when stock options began to form ever-larger portions of remuneration for agents to more closely align their interests to the interests of owners (Jensen and Meckling, 1976). The conversion of agents into owners, and concomitant wealth accretion, greatly expanded the size of the executive class and further separated management from workers. Remuneration via stock options led to a much stronger financial focus, and, coupled with many new business performance metrics, resulted in more forceful downward control and direction, and concomitantly less upward communication and reduced employee engagement. Overall, executives grew less interested in what workers had to say, and the relationship between management and labor became ever-more servile. This created conditions that were the opposite of what is required for Lean – no doubt a fortuitous development for executives and an unfortunate circumstance for workers, as it became much more difficult for workers to be heard and to advance their ideas or economic interests, singly or in unison.

To get managers at each level of a hierarchy to accept a suggestion or new idea, workers must "pay" managers (owners) through subservience: acts of fealty, manners, decorum, verification, and certification, all displayed in good form at the requisite times. What develops is a quasi-merit-based system exclusive to owners (executives) but a dense, difficult, time-consuming, and irritating political system that non-owners (workers) are forced to navigate. Thus, the merits of Lean, however numerous or potent they may be, are quickly and easily extinguished by owners' distinctive or shared prerogatives at every level of the management hierarchy. Characteristically, management may allow selected tools and methods of Lean to be used in the furtherance of owners' interests or to mollify workers or other interested parties. But Lean, as a system to replace classical management practice, is terminated through owners' well-established forceful mechanisms of control designed to perpetuate their preferred traditions and benefits. Classical political economy plays a central role in the mechanism of control to maintain and expand the executive class and its culture.

Certain core economic ideas developed in 19th century England quickly became fixed in the minds of business owners as morally superior and have remained intact to this day, as economic theory has steadily built upon these foundational ideas. Key concepts in classical political economy were eagerly accepted by owners because they confirmed their biases and legitimized their interests (war, hunting, sports, and devout observances). The key concepts and criticisms of the concepts are as follows (Wayland, 1885; Ingram, 1888; Veblen, 1904):

Economic Man: This fictitious abstraction of mankind removes all other human variables to simplify investigation and analysis of economic phenomena. However, critics contend that because God did not create such a man, none can actually exist, thereby negating economics as a true science. Nevertheless, economic man was successfully established as an exemplary model for business owners to emulate.

Self-Interest: The pursuit of self-interest and personal (material) gain were seen as secondary motives to one's work. The prime motive for one's work is service, self-sacrifice, to fellow human beings and the community – this is the sole characteristic that constitutes a "noble" or "great profession." Self-sacrifice must be embedded in business, not "economic man," whose self-interested quest for gain is happily pursued in zero-sum fashion.

Profit-Seeking: This was seen as a base motive, one that grossly conflicted with the virtue of self-sacrifice. Money-gain was not viewed as true gain. The number of happy human beings was seen as the measure of richness. Profit-seeking brought wealth to owners and poverty to workers, and made it difficult for workers to feel affiliated with an organization knowing that owners may cast them aside at any moment, thereby fracturing human and community relations.

Laissez-Faire: The concept of "let it go," self-regulation, was seen by critics as "the devil's philosophy," an excuse for leaders to avoid their responsibilities to lead, to avoid work, and to avoid providing for the community to sustain life. Relatedly, there was strong moral disagreement with the idea that wealth unjustly derived is economically equivalent to wealth justly derived, the latter resulting in great disparities in wealth that disadvantaged workers and community interests.

Natural Rights: Human being's intrinsic or natural rights to life, liberty, and property, where ownership is given by one's own work or by trade or by inheritance. Particularly, freedom by an owner to do as he wishes with his property, the business, and all material and human resources contained within it – often to the detriment of the community.

Early critics of political economy – those who were closer in time to its creation – grounded their criticism in facets of daily living with reference to the virtuous characteristics of mankind created by God and as informed by religious writings and human survival. They were deeply skeptical of these five elements of political economy, and questioned claims made as to its standing as a science, likening it instead to astrology. It is noteworthy that pioneers of political economy lacked scientific training and were held in open contempt by actual scientists.

The critics viewed science as something that helps people labor for that which supports or improves life. Political economy, with its acceptance of zero-sum outcomes did the opposite and therefore resulted in destruction. The religious overtones of the critiques clearly indicate that such outcomes were new and unwelcome additions to human existence. Thus, ideas central to political economy were lacking in the moral dimensions integral to human ideals and human existence as bestowed by God.

In different ways and to varying degrees, the five concepts were seen as anti-human, un-human, or working against human interests given by God; e.g. of cooperation, community, work, livelihood, and life. Respect and service, self-sacrifice (unselfishness), are intertwined. Remove self-sacrifice, and one removes respect. Thus, the foundation is laid for trickery and deceit in pursuit of one's own interests, which leads straight to destruction: "The motive of self-interest leads men to wrong-doing more often than to right-doing, and should therefore be replaced by the motive of public interest" (Cooke-Taylor, 1891).

The critics decried people who accepted these five economic ideas with no critical thought, particularly those that exempted humanity from money-making. They viewed elements of classical economics as deeply disrespectful of people. It corrupts and compromises the virtuous gifts that God gave to humans, and reduces God's influence and lowers His rank. People were the true source of wealth, and service the true purpose of one's work.

Unable to objectively judge the value of the human or his work, businessmen found it easier to judge all matters in relation to money – "pecuniary interests" (Veblen, 1904). These five economic ideas soon became a habit of mind at scale and became immune to criticism or re-consideration. They became entrenched for nearly two centuries and could not be controverted no matter how cogent the argument.

Work, enmeshed with economics, must develop one's humanity, not remove it. The political economy concepts coupled with complex machinery were a detriment to the further development of workers' humanity, impairing their ability to absorb the world around them and bring forth imagination and creativity to their work, and was, therefore, soul-destroying. Borrowing from Veblen (1904), one can sum up by saying:

"[Economics], their master, is no respecter of persons and knows neither morality nor dignity nor prescriptive rights, divine or human."

Stock options and executive pay some 200 to 300 times the earnings of workers are a post-modern creation based on 19th century political economy, and which reinforces the superior rank of the owner-executive class and diminishes the work, honor, and respectability of laborers (wage and salary earners). Political economy profoundly reinforces the tradition of tying wealth to honor and rank, and therefore anyone who does not possess wealth lacks honor and rank. As wealth confers superior rank, it also confers a superior mind, and superior moral character in business and in life. Lean, utilizing the brainpower of workers and requiring productive engagement by executives, interferes with the habits and techniques of superior minds. Workers using their brainpower – to think about their work and improve it – unnecessarily diminish respected totems of executive class honor and rank such as fealty, decorum, etiquette, etc.

The economic basis under which Toyota's production system developed and evolved over time can be summarized simply as relieving the suffering of the people in a society, regardless of class, and striving to achieve balance and social harmony (Morris-Suzuki, 1989). It is just and moral to join both society and wealth. In contrast, it should be obvious that classical political economy has, as a common practical outcome, to create suffering through wealth disparity and is apathetic to balance and social harmony. The separation of society and wealth are recognized as beneficial features, not as flaws. The practice of Lean management, injected into businesses whose executives are anchored in classical political economy, is destined to struggle for years if not quickly fail, regardless of whether Lean is practiced in partial or full form. Successful adoption of Lean in its full form requires executives to modify their understanding of classical political economy – something that few executives realize they need to do or are willing to do.

Essential Learning

Advancing within a hierarchy towards inclusion in the executive class requires learning and mastering three subjects, not all of which are equal in importance. The subjects are: technical job requirements, class-related protocols, and, at the highest levels of the hierarchy, the Wealth Creation Playbook (Table 1-2).

Failure to master the class-related protocols is a far more serious problem than failure to master the technical aspects of administrative work or the Wealth Creation Playbook, the latter of which is essentially trivial and executed by subordinates and proficient subcontractors. Nevertheless, the Wealth Creation Playbook is a relevant subject in this study because its use is invariably said by CEOs to result in improved business performance (see Note 3). Furthermore, the Wealth Creation Playbook clearly shows executives are far more concerned with financial efficiency than they are with process efficiency, and that they view the two as incompatible. First, we begin with class-related protocols.

Table 1-2: CEOs Wealth Creation Playbook

Method for Improving Business Results	Degree of Difficulty (10 = highest)	Time to Execute (years)
Layoffs	1	<1
Hire New Managers	1	<<1
Close Facilities	1	<1
Stock Buy-Backs	1	1-3
Acquisition	2	1-2
Merger	2	1-2
Divestiture / Spinoff	2	1
Change Incentive Compensation	1	<1
Develop New Products	2	1-2
Develop New Markets	3	1-3
Discontinue Products / Services	1	<<1
Reduce / Increase Debt	1	<1
Change Accounting Method	2	1
Incorporate Offshore (inversion)	2	1
Consolidate Operations	2	1-2
Technology / Automation / Digitization	1	1-2
Outsource	2	1-2
Squeeze Suppliers on Prices	1	<1
Price Cuts / Price Increases	1	<<1
Sales Promotions	2	1
Patent Term Extension	2	1-2
Budget Cuts	1	<1
Seek Lower Taxes and Less Regulation	2	1-3

The many professional and personal benefits of hierarchical advancement create a powerful incentive to master all class-related protocols – particularly Devout Observances – which is nearly an all-consuming education that usually begins at the mid-level manager position and continues up to the CEO and Chairman of the Board. Being an all-consuming education, there can never be any time to learn Lean. What must instead be learned to survive and prosper?

Those who are one level above in status and wealth are the models that those who are one level below must emulate if they hope to advance. The next higher level becomes the target condition to strive for. Upon careful observation, the class-related protocols become clear, as does the mindset and canon of morals and honorifics associated with the executive class. The essential learnings begin with these:

- Exemption from manual (productive/useful) labor
- Earn respect by using and abusing others
- Unambiguous treatment of workers as subordinates
- Give orders and assure their faithful execution
- Swift and visible punishment for not following orders or for doing poor work
- Brash self-promotion; attribute the work of others to one's self

The requirement of the higher-level executive is for the next lower level executive to exhibit the requisite subservience. Obtaining subservience from others is honorific, while those who exhibit unquestioning subservience, in good form of course, are considered more reputable and of greater worth than those subordinates who consider themselves equal to the next higher level. Worth is markedly expanded when, in addition to precisely understanding relational status, the subordinate is skilled at inflicting ridicule, pain, or punishment to others on their superior's behalf.

Another essential learning to master at each step up the hierarchy is how to waste time, for in this there is great honor to be had. In addition, the wasting of time favors the interests of the executive class. Wasting time takes on two forms:

- Assuring an increasingly non-productive existence for one's self
- Running out the clock on workers' wants and desires

Non-productive consumption of time is a marker of one's status in the hierarchy. The non-productive use of time, day in and day out, signifies high social standing. As time is money, one's ability to waste time is an expression of one's wealth and ability to freely waste it with impunity. This includes meetings, business travel, delayed action, indecision, and any other tactic that serves the purpose of assuring a non-productive existence.

Running out the clock is a separate but related phenomenon, evidence of which is plainly visible. For example, executives meet periodically with workers, but invariably without pen or paper to record notes or actions to take. To document interactions with workers is a grave mistake for it generates a record of problems in one's area of responsibility.

Further, action items dictated by workers disrupt the executive's efforts to be non-productive. The only disruption in leisure time allowed comes from above, not from below. It is also unwise to delegate action items to an assistant because they may someday work for a rival and expose their former superiors' deficiencies, ineptitudes, and failures. Finally, responding to workers by way of action items represent weakness, drudgery, and otherwise ignoble work.

In the case of words and associated actions, there exists a law of executive decorum pertaining to their relationship with workers which states that an executive must say they will do a lot, but actually do very little. As one rises through the hierarchy, an executive must say ever-more but do ever-less for workers at each step along the way. This informs all workers in a department or functional area that their leader can use words as objects that serve no useful purpose in the workplace. And it makes clear to all, on a continuing basis, who serves whom.

The executive perspective of workers is embodied in the classic phrase: "Don't think, just do what you are told." This perspective has evolved over time and is embodied in a variant the old phrase: "Do your job and improve your job." The expectation is that workers will find and use any tool to help increase the quality of their work and productivity. In contrast, executives' perspective of themselves has remained constant: "Do the job but don't improve the job." Executives, in furtherance of good standing, wealth, and reputation, must do nothing but increase their sacred non-productive time (Figure 1-2). Inaction is good governance.

Workers' role is to create comfort and idle time for executives. When this does not happen, executives become agitated and upset. They are quick to anger when problems arise because their leisure time has been disrupted, with the potential for loss of honor and status, and political attacks from rivals that threaten one's hegemony and wealth. Blame and other forms of disrespect are the preferred response because they clarify and reinforce the servile basis of the manager-worker relationship.

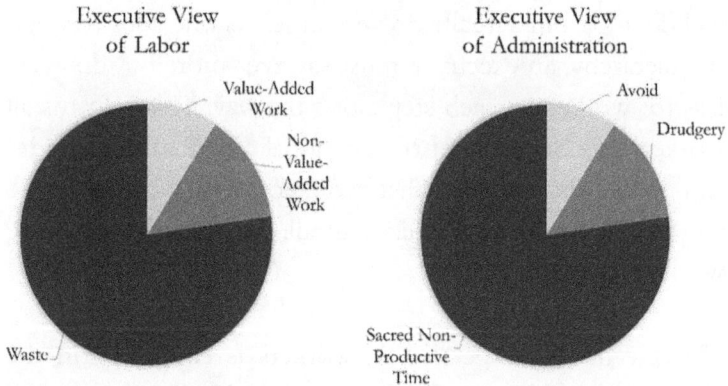

Figure 1-2. Differences in perspective of the role and contribution of labor (left) [Ohno, 1988]) and executives (right). For labor, waste, activities that add cost but create no value, must be eliminated and value-added work increased. For executives, waste (sacred non-productive time) must be increased.

Development of these essential skills, beginning early in one's management career, create habits of mind and actions that preserve traditions and maintain the present state of affairs. The skills required to do so are highly valued and considered heroic and honorific, and enshrined in the Wealth Creation Playbook. A habit developed early and applied for many years is difficult to break, assuming one would want to do so. Said another way, a habit put into motion tends to stay in motion, following a consistent direction established long ago though education, observation, work experience, mentoring, or combinations thereof. Habits are easy to add and difficult to subtract. Lean requires the subtraction of nearly all habits of executive mind and action.

Superimposed upon these essential learnings is an elaborate system of class-related protocols and rituals pertaining to Devout Observances. Specifically, fealty, manners, etiquette, decorum, emulation, flattery, temperament, demeanor, and so on. In addition, there are matters of erudition pertaining to appearance, taste, style, dress, food, drink, art, decorations, humor and wit, entertainment, and the like. All must be displayed or conducted in good form as determined by the next level in the hierarchy. Fluency in these protocols is the top prerequisite for advancement, as any shortcomings in technical job performance can be rectified by other means. This underscores the significance of personal interaction and subservience as the perpetual test of acceptance among the occupants of each rung of the hierarchy.

It is apparent that there is much new and continuous learning that must occur and which fully occupies one's time as executives advance stepwise through the hierarchy. There is no time to learn Lean, even if the desire to do so existed. That, coupled with management churn – a new boss every few years – places unremitting demands to continue learning in the direction of previously established habits. Further, the accretion of honorable habits that strengthen and perpetuate class-related protocols are revered, while those which conflict with it constitute debasements that are incompatible with one's standing and executive-class interests.

Another essential learning is the Wealth Creation Playbook (Table 1-2) because it is held in high esteem for its ability to provide its practitioners with conspicuous wins, wealth, and social recognition. Lean, on the other hand, is not known by the executive class to do that. Therefore, it is incumbent on those who rise to the top of the hierarchy to use the Wealth Creation Playbook to preserve traditions and lines of authority, and to create wealth for the executive class. To do otherwise is to bring dishonor to one's self and to others in the executive class.

The Wealth Creation Playbook is the accredited source for executive action. Accreditation is conferred through the long heritage of its use by prior generations of executives. To use other methods is to disparage, discredit, and dishonor those prior generations as well as one's self. Furthermore, the use of the Wealth Creation Playbook is ubiquitous, which confirms it as the accredited and dignified source of executive action. It is the truth. Lean, however, is unaccredited in the eyes of executives and it therefore brings dishonor to those who employ it.

The Wealth Creation Playbook reflects the value placed upon action, as expressed in the degree of difficulty to implement (low) and the speed of implementation (fast), that must take place when opportunities arise or when circumstances place the business at risk. Lean has great difficulty competing on the merits of ease and speed because of the slow pace at which new habits of mind and practice are learned. Even if Lean did not suffer such shortcomings, there is no deep record of tradition, honor, and dignity associated with it.

Taboo Learning

Taboo learning is anything perceived by the executive class as being associated with manual labor; activities normally performed by workers. Yet to learn Lean, one must participate in improvement activities. The most potent learning is achieved through participation in shop floor kaizen. This is how Toyota's twin principles, "Continuous Improvement" and "Respect for People" are applied and understood. Knowledge is deepened each time one participates in kaizen, usually 3 to 5 days in duration. Soon, kaizen participants discover a truth: You're never done learning.

Kaizen teams are typically comprised of hourly and salary workers and supervisors from different functional areas. Occasionally, mid-level managers participate, often more to satisfy curiosity than to learn. Shop floor kaizen is mostly manual labor. Kaizen to improve office processes does not dirty hands in the same way as shop floor kaizen, though it remains a type of manual labor and presents other related problems for executives. Specific reasons why kaizen is taboo learning include:

Interaction with Workers

- Executives must personally engage with other kaizen team members for several days as equals, not as executives. It includes taking direction from the kaizen team leader, who is a worker or supervisor.

Manual Labor

- Team members analyze a work process and perform manual labor to improve the process. They move equipment and machines, run machines, make prototypes, test out ideas, and so on. It is hands-on work.

Uniform

- Manual labor requires executives to disrobe; to take off their expensive uniform and jewelry and instead wear clothes that hourly employees wear; i.e. t-shirt and blue jeans.

Learning

- Participation in even one shop floor kaizen normally results in the stark realization that one is not nearly as smart as they thought they were.

Discomfort

- The executive class values comfort and views their pursuit of comfort as honorable. Kaizen causes deep discomfort – mental, physical, and social discomfort.

Participation in kaizen diminishes executive status and authority temporarily and for longer periods – a risk that few are willing to take. That one is never done learning is a truth that the executive class scrupulously avoids because it clouds their thinking and complicates application of the Wealth Creation Playbook. But, most importantly, executives are too busy learning other things to participate in kaizen. Whether in the context of kaizen or not, discomfort instantly materializes when a worker tries to help an executive learn something new or innovative. This is obnoxious and backwards to the established laws of executive prerogative in which executives tell workers what to do.

The performance of manual labor by the executive class is something to abstain from because it is perceived as odious, unclean, menial, and identifiable with debasement, inferiority, weakness, and dishonor. Kaizen is synonymous with discomfort. It is ignoble work unworthy of their personal involvement. Kaizen induces a loss of executive honorifics and is therefore vulgar and undignified. Furthermore, kaizen is offensive to the executive class because it reveals imperfections and defects in that which they admire and regard as a thing of purified beauty: the company.

It is taboo for executives to even know or understand any details associated with manual labor. Mere knowledge of the details of manual work are fully as offensive as having to perform the manual work. Kaizen participation is therefore instinctively and morally objectionable, and participation must be avoided. As a result, the executive class never learns

Lean, which is not something they care about anyway. They will, however, rapidly adopt the language of Lean and cheerlead workers in their efforts to learn Lean and improve shop and office processes. Speeches to employees extolling the importance of Lean to the company are firmly in the domain of noble executive work that is entirely theirs to perform. However important Lean may be, all ignoble work must be delegated – even at the risk of hypocrisy, which is an insignificant price to pay to avoid debasement and which bears no consequences anyway.

Under these common conditions, the magnitude of the business results that can be achieved with Lean are severely limited. As the business results fail to accrue, there is no one to blame but the workers; blaming subordinates being among the honorific duties of the superior class. However, poor business results from Lean are far less important than preserving traditions from the ancient past (tribalism, division of labor) and near-past (19th century political economy). And any shortcoming in financial results can be quickly regained though the application of the Wealth Creation Playbook.

It appears that for these reasons, Womack and Jones' Lean has, for decades, de-emphasized dirty-hands kaizen and instead focused on clean-hands improvement methods (Figure 1-1). But, to no avail, as executives quickly recognized that clean-hands improvement is also grotesque and morally prohibitive, and causes them much discomfort through awareness of the existence of distasteful defects and repugnant manual process details as embodied in value stream maps, A3 reports, gemba walks, and coaching. More generally, Lean fractures executive decorum and compromises executive privilege. So, why do it? In fact, they cannot do it.

Manual labor is what the executive class purchases, it is not what they personally do – especially not in their place of business where a loss in status and authority cannot be tolerated and which is difficult to repair. The few executives who regularly participate in or lead kaizens are naturally perceived by their peers to be deviants within the executive class for having broken sacred covenants. While they may not be banished from the class, they lack influence when it comes to Lean and perhaps other things as well.

Advancement Kata and Wealth Kata

In Lean, structured practice patterns or routines, called "katas," have gained popularity as a method for learning how to think scientifically and how to make iterative progress towards achieving challenging goals (Rother, 2009). There are two types of katas: An "improvement kata" (Figure 1-3), and a "coaching kata," which is a practice routine for teaching improvement katas.

Learners and coaches interact with one another daily to slowly embed within the organization a scientific way of thinking for recognizing and solving problems. The fundamental idea behind kata is to create a higher performing organization by improving employees' problem-solving capabilities and abilities to attain the challenging goals set by their superiors.

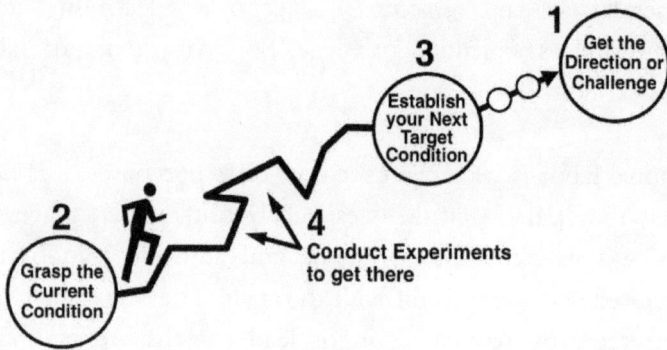

Figure 1-3. The four-step pattern of the improvement kata. Step 4, experiments, follows the pattern of the Plan-Do-Check-Act cycle. Source: *Toyota Kata Practice Guide*. Used with permission (Rother, 2017).

The improvement kata is a method for learning how to learn. All employees, managers, and executives are presumed to have a need to learn. And subordinates at each level of the organization have a direct superior whose role it is, in part, to teach them how to practice their improvement kata through coaching cycles. In its actual practice, however, organizations that adopt kata routines often limit it to just one pairwise relationship closest to the working level: workers (hourly or salary learners) and front-line supervisors (coaches).

The improvement kata consists of four steps (Rother, 2009):

1. Get the direction or challenge
2. Grasp the current situation
3. Establish you next target condition
4. Conduct experiments to get there

The coaching kata asks five questions (Rother, 2009):

1. What is the target condition?
2. What is the actual condition now?
3. What obstacles do you think are preventing you from reaching the target condition?
4. What is your next step?
5. How quickly can we go and see what we have learned from taking that step?

When the improvement and coaching katas are limited to workers and front-line supervisors, one can conclude that mid-level managers up through to the executive level have different learning and coaching interests. The desired learning at higher levels pertain to advancement and wealth, while coaching – mentoring, actually – if done, is highly selective so as not to impinge too much upon one's sacred non-productive time. Thus, the focus of executive's attention is the advancement kata and the wealth kata.

The advancement kata is practiced by managers who seek greater responsibility and advancement. As is clear from the previous sections of this study, the advancement kata does not utilize a scientific approach to learning. Instead, it uses social, political, and economic approaches to learning. Instead of learning based on science, learning is based on people; specifically, the people who ranker higher in the hierarchy. These are two vastly different bases for learning.

The advancement kata consists of only two steps:

1. Get the direction or challenge

2. Get there

The reason there are only two steps is because once the direction or challenge has been given, it is coincident with the target. The current situation is embodied in step 2, "get there." Step four is disallowed because experiments take time and engender the likelihood of multiple failures. So, two steps are all that is required to improve and achieve challenging goals – two steps to win. Admission to the next step in the hierarchy is allowed only after proficiency is demonstrated in steps one and two of the advancement kata.

The wealth kata is practiced by those who have advanced to the CEO, president, and vice-president levels. The word "wealth" principally means monetary wealth, but also includes status, standing, and reputation. The wealth kata also asks five questions:

1. How do we control the market?
2. How do we expand profit margins?
3. How do we increase the stock price?
4. By when do we need to achieve this?
5. Who or what do we need to help us?

Wealth Creation Playbook answers the first four questions, hence its sacred value in executive decision-making and action. Question five normally takes the form of a new executive hire or the engagement of an expensive top-tier consulting firm. Instead of "coaching cycles" there are "wealth cycles" in which the target for wealth must increase inexorably from one period, monthly, quarterly, or annually, to the next. That is continuous wealth improvement. From this we can see that one thing is clear: The goal remains constant – easy work, comfort, and wealth. Even Lean's supposed savior, "the burning platform" – a condition of severe financial distress – has proven to be no match for either the Wealth Creation Playbook or executive culture.

Forever attached to Lean is an unfortunate and weighty attribute: It conflicts with executive's established understanding of hierarchical advancement, wealth creation and wealth accumulation, as well as heroic deeds and honorific attributes. This makes Lean impure and unworthy of executive attention (Table 1-1).

Sanctity of Higher Education

Whether one is a graduate of a prestigious Ivy League institution or a third-tier public institution, the education of the executive class is sacred and must not be disturbed. The education was expensive in money, time, and effort, and it is therefore reputable and trustworthy. If one is taught how to solve a problem in school, then one must solve the problem the same way out of school – at least until shown otherwise.

Once in the workplace, if one sees a higher-level executive solve a problem a certain way, derived from their higher education, then they invariably solve the problem the same way when they become the higher-level executive. That is the standard. One must not question things that have no need to be questioned. These are expressions of good taste, decorum, and Devout Observance.

Higher education is apparel or dress for the intellect. It is internal couture that compliments external couture; a hidden aesthetic that has spiritual energy, practical value, and social worth. Graduating from the best schools drapes ennobling haute couture onto the intellect, which intensifies reputation, honor, success, and superiority. The finely crafted apparel of both mind and body make it impractical for the executive class to engage in productive labor, which itself is further evidence of success and good fortune.

Completion of higher education is the endpoint. The knowledge conveyed by professors who are expert in teaching and in their fields of study establishes worth. The tradition is to use what was learned, and not learned, whether the field of study is business, economics, arts, science, or engineering. It is one's duty to solve a problem as prescribed. Learn only what the professor knows; what the professor knows, you now know. It is a form of property conferred to graduates that, when put into use, enhances one's repute. It soon matures into a habit of mind that is virtually impossible to breach. Because it is honorable, there is a great reluctance to give up the teachings in toto. The Wealth Creation Playbook reflects the teachings, both in higher education and in business practice, incorporating modifications that suit the needs and comfort of the executive class. The Wealth Creation Playbook is recognized as both good and right and accepted as the canon of profitable knowledge.

Because the teachings are both sacred and ubiquitous, there is immense social pressure to conform. There is an equally immense desire to avoid unwanted scrutiny or unfavorable commentary from others in the executive class such as: "Was your Ivy League education not good enough?" or "Don't you think this will hurt your reputation?" Adopting Lean in its full form as a management system calls for elaborate explanation to one's peers, yet Lean is almost impossible to explain because it is something that must be experienced first-hand. Few want to provide detailed rationale or justifications to their peers because failure is all but certain; there is nothing one can say to convince their peers of the merits of Lean. In adopting Lean, there is a risk of falling out of favor with one's peers and alma mater. To adopt Lean is to disrespect one's professors and the body of knowledge meticulously built by countless scholars over time, as well as the school and the university.

In Lean, higher education is seen as only the starting point because one is never done learning. The desire to continue learning that which can only be learned on the shop or office floor is more sacred than knowledge imparted to students by professors; what the professor does not know, you now know. Questioning everything is revered because this continuously feeds the human learning, creativity, and innovation required for prosperity to flourish and long-term business success. Know-how, developed through individual and team efforts, trying new things, using derivatives of the scientific method – kaizen, improvement kata, Plan-Do-Check-Act cycle, A3 reports, etc. – and the ability to simplify processes are truer measures of worth. Yet, to the executive class, the learning that Lean offers comes from unqualified sources. It is a cheapened education that is both unworthy and indigestible (see Note 4). The formal and informal education of the executive class fulfills the need and sets the standard. It conforms to requirements and its survival proves its worth and fitness. There is no need for change.

Lean puts the executive class in numerous difficult binds from nearly every direction. It creates business, professional, and personal problems that they cannot easily manage or control. Hence, they must abstain from a full embrace of Lean management. Any interest in Lean must therefore be limited to selected tools and methods which cause them no difficulties and which could possibly make small positive contributions to business profitability and performance. Full commitment to Lean management is left to the tiny cadre of deviant CEOs who wish to pursue success by a different method.

Protecting and Preserving Institutions

The executive class is more than just a class. It is an institution rich in traditions whose members seek to assure its survival through the perpetuation of its interests. Being an institution rooted in the past, its interests will naturally conflict with the needs and requirements at any point in time which marks the present. As it is slow to adapt, the institution and its members will disfavor the advancement of progressive transformation of businesses that they have authority over. Views and practices that one might perceive as archaic are seen by others as current, providing needed order, and benefitting a large population of society. Progress, it can be argued, is being made, slow though it might seem, or that stasis or even retrogression is a more favorable condition because it benefits society at-large.

As an institution charged with protecting another institution, business, the executive class must insulate itself and business from the forces that would alter either institution. Therefore, they must firmly embrace a worldview that serves its purpose, to preserve the past, which, as time passes, becomes ever-more theoretical in its construction than practical. Unimpeachable evidence of innovation in management thinking and practice must be rejected – not for ill motives, but simply for the preservation of traditions, honor, and respect. Their obligation, conscious or unconscious, is to preserve the past, not to advancement and innovation. Devoutness to traditions assures survival of both self (class) and culture.

Lean, a modern innovation brought to reality by workers in conjunction with productive executive labor, is not something whose merits the executive class want to acknowledge or associate itself with. Lean is of a different, lower class. The few, therefore, disallow advancement of the many. And so, as the executive class views Lean as unacceptable, the classes below absorb their influence and feel likewise, thereby allowing the sacred institutions to remain strong and vibrant.

As the successful Lean CEO Art Byrne has long said, "Everything must change" when it comes to Lean transformation (Byrne, 2012). True as these words are, they are nonetheless thoroughly repulsive and completely distasteful to the executive class. It requires them to do the opposite of what they are obliged to do: protect and preserve their institutions. Changing everything is impractical, painful, bothersome, and rife with complications, discomfort, and objectionable consequences. The mental effort and energy needed is far beyond reason, and it impinges upon their sacred non-productive time and perfected practice of judging all matters in relation to money. Lean is a disturbance that nullifies the established order and habits of mind, and is therefore detrimental to the executive class's interests. One must leave well enough alone as the established order is good and right, and it delivers much-valued clarity and certainty.

Summary

"We've got great ideas but we are still struggling to get the world's managers to adopt them." (Womack, 2017a)

As this study has attempted to show, Womack's struggle is far greater than he apparently realized. Mere changes in strategy and tactics are unlikely to dislodge executives from their view of Lean as antithetical or irrelevant (see Note 5) to their class and cultural interests. It seems that Womack, a political scientist, and his colleague, Dan Jones, an economist, should realize that better than anyone. Perhaps the Womack and Jones team of sociologists comprehend the substance of what this study conveys and chose to not address it, or they were unaware of it and believed that success can be achieved despite it. One wonders how doing so serves the interests of their customers and the Lean community at-large.

The executive class also has "great ideas" – many great ideas that have withstood the test of time to which devotion and sanctity are firmly attached. Far longer in time than progressive management, which comes and goes inconsistently, and which is subject to such large variation in understanding and widespread dilution in practice as to render it deficient if not functionally useless. This too is fortuitous for executives and an unfortunate circumstance for workers and the Lean movement.

The proponents of Lean have long assumed that executives would freely accept Lean though the combined presentation of data, facts, logical arguments, and by showing real-world examples of the magic of Lean. Yet, the Wealth Creation Playbook represents the accredited system that, through its diligent application, produces wealth and honor almost without fail (see Note 6). The executive class rewards one another with honor for adhering to the tenets which uphold the Wealth Creation Playbook and its frequent use as indicators of the application of power and control. The Playbook will remain in force and relevant far into the future (see Note 7), despite its apparent drag on economic and human development.

Progressive Lean management is a populist, quasi-democratic management practice. To adopt Lean means to reverse honored traditions and discard habits of thought that have long yielded favorable business and personal results. It seems impractical to expect that anything more than a small number of wayward CEOs (and their boards of directors) would happily adopt Lean management in its full form and bring dishonor and decay to the executive class. If one wishes to be reputable in the class, then one must be respectful of the established rules and follow them meticulously.

The continued dominance of 19th century political economy in executive thought and action has had a thoroughly stultifying effect on their ability to consider Lean as a management system that is better suited for current and future times. The apparent solution is to replace archaic economic ideas with new ones that are consistent with Lean and the needs of humanity and its communities. But, who would lead such an effort and how much influence could they exert on the executive class? This will take time, perhaps well-spent, but new economic ideas consistent with Lean may arrive after entrenchment of the robotics and artificial intelligence and concomitant displacement of labor – a clear alignment with 19th century classical political economy – when Lean might be, in either fact or perception, no longer relevant to large corporations.

In decades past, labor unions were influential and successful in representing workers' interests. That is not the case today. A resurrection of labor unions, by means unknown, could compel executives to adopt Lean in full form as a management system and practice it to high effect. However, labor unions have a long history of hostility towards progressive management, revealing an abject failure by generations of national and local union leaders to understand Lean's motives and benefits to workers as well as management, much to the satisfaction of the executive class. Labor unions, in their effort to improve workers' lives and livelihoods, have missed what could have been their greatest asset. If resurrected, labor unions would most likely continue in the direction of previously established habits which have been largely defeated.

The present study offers no easy solution to this difficult problem. Yet, it illustrates the perils of preconceptions (assumptions) such as using various logical and rational means to persuade a prominent class of wealthy and influential people whose interests are far more complex and interdependent than is immediately visible or which they are willing to voluntarily reveal. This study has exposed the complexity and interdependent features of executive culture and established the challenge ahead for those who still hope to gain widespread acceptance of Lean management by the corporate executive class. They should keep these words by Taiichi Ohno in mind as they move forward (Ohno and Mito, 1988):

"...we are doomed to failure if we do not initiate a daily destruction of our various preconceptions."

The context of this quote is process improvement in manufacturing, but these words apply equally to improving the process for gaining wider acceptance of Lean management among the executives of large corporations, which has been clearly burdened by numerous preconceptions.

Finally, the author wishes to again remind readers that the aim of this chapter was a Veblenesque socioeconomic interpretation of a curious phenomenon in business as it relates to wealth, economics, labor, and human relations (see Notes 8-12). It exposed the deep conflicts and grinding friction that exists between classical management and modern Lean management, from which will rise new opportunities. *Vivere est cogitare.*

Questions to Reflect On

- Do you listen to and respect executives who resist the change to Lean? Do you label them as bad leaders for resisting Lean? Does it make sense to do that after reading this chapter?

- What other bedrock assumptions need to be tested to determine if they are valid?

- What can be done to lessen the strong influence of classical political economy?

- How can Lean be made to function better within fundamentally inhospitable corporate environments (Table 1-1)?

- In what ways can Lean compete better on the basis of ease and speed (Table 1-2)?

- What more can be done to close the perception gap among executives that financial efficiency (Table 1-2) and process efficiency are incompatible?

- If Lean is fundamentally incompatible with big company executive culture, where should efforts to advance Lean be focused?

- What can the successful Lean CEOs do individually or as a team that they have not already done to influence CEOs of large corporations?

- Based on what you read in this chapter, how would you start a discussion on Lean management with an executive team that is: a) unfamiliar with Lean and b) familiar with Lean (first 10 minutes)?

- Referring to Note 7, if questioned by a CEO on these points, how would you respond?

Notes

1. As a Veblenesque socioeconomic interpretation, this chapter uses colorful language and strong rhetoric that can easily be misinterpreted as unduly provocative or offensive. That is not the intent of the style of writing. This chapter could also be misperceived as class warfare, a strawman argument, a jeremiad, or an opinion piece. It is none of these. Misunderstandings and misinterpretations overshadow the critical thinking, first-hand experience, and empirical evidence that are the foundation of this work. The chapter should be carefully read in the context of the problem statement to grasp the sources and consequences of executive's resistance to Lean. And keep in mind the limited claim made in this chapter: It "...offers a *plausible* and detailed understanding of the culture and causal relationships that delineate executive resistance to Lean."

2. Veblen's taxonomy reflects the almost entirely male-dominated executive class of the mid- to late 1800s. While the executive class is less male-dominated today, Veblen's taxonomy is retained in this study because it continues to reflect the preoccupations of executive culture today, whether the executive is male or female. In addition, the taxonomy remains valid today and in the future given the continued use of the Wealth Creation Playbook.

3. Institutional shareholders, boards of directors, investment bankers, corporate raiders, and potential acquirers exert strong influences on corporate officers. The fastest and easiest way to satisfy their interests is by using the Wealth Creation Playbook.

4. It is commonly observed that Lean devotees believe they possess superior knowledge of right and wrong ways of thinking and of doing things, and hence fashion themselves as guardians of the Truth (e.g. "the gemba is the truth"). This is perceived unfavorably by the executive class as not knowing one's station in the hierarchy and clear violations of decorum and subservience. Lean thinkers' well-intentioned efforts to help executives is viewed as confrontational and regarded as an affront to their status, knowledge, and experience.

5. Since 1988, Lean production has blossomed into numerous niche applications – e.g. Lean human resources, Lean product development, Lean supply chain, Lean media, Lean IT, Lean maintenance, Lean project management, Lean office, Lean recruitment, Lean startup, Lean sales, Lean customer development, Lean safety, Lean teaching, and so on. To the extent that executives are aware of this atomization of Lean, it cannot be comforting to them because it suggests that an ever-larger larger devotion of corporate resources are required for Lean which, in turn, detracts from wealth and contributes to making Lean vacuous and irrelevant in their eyes. The fundamental executive need is for workers to do their job, and, more recently, to improve their work, regardless of the tools used. Failure to do so is quickly remedied as shown in Table 1-2.

6. For many years, Lean was proffered to executives as new capitalist method for "wealth creation" (Womack and Jones, 1996). To a CEO, methods for creating wealth have long existed in classical management practice. Therefore, they do not have a need for a replacement method to create wealth.

Apparently, the two are seen as trading 100 kilograms of gold (classical management practice) for 10,000 kilograms of silver (Lean management system). Their value is equivalent (minus transaction costs), so why bother? Will proffering Lean as a corporate strategy and as a people-centered management system (Ballé et al., 2017) result in a different outcome? Are executives, trained in classical management practice, interested in uniting strategy and execution? Are they interested in a new people-centered management system? It remains to be seen.

7. The Wealth Creation Playbook will remain in force and relevant far into the future because, in its 30 years of existence, Lean transformation has a poor record of success, where success is defined as achieving something close to Toyota's management practice and corporate culture (Byrne, 2012). It also has a terrible record of sustainability due to frequent changes in management and periodic changes in company ownership. The success rate for Lean transformation is widely believed to be just three to five percent for companies of all sizes. CEOs who are aware of this would question why they should invest in Lean transformation (combination of all necessary resources) if it has a greater than 90 percent chance of failure. From the CEOs perspective, the return on investment is likely to be a large negative number. This perspective would likely exist even if the success rate was 50 percent. A 50 percent chance of failure is also unattractive. Alternatively, a very high success rate for Lean transformation could indicate to executives that Lean offers no competitive advantage – everyone is doing it – so they will seek competitive advantage by other means. Finally, the Wealth Creation

Playbook is perceived by CEOs and major shareholders as a "sure thing," while Lean transformation is rife with uncertainty – which CEOs detest. Proffering Lean as a corporate strategy (Byrne, 2012; Ballé et al., 2017), does not seem to change these dynamics overall, but it will likely appeal to a small number of CEOs.

8. Whenever one discusses what leaders do or not do, there is a high likelihood of it being interpreted as an "us-versus-them" invective. That would be a misinterpretation of this chapter. Occupying a leadership position means one freely accepts responsibility for their thinking and decisions. This chapter merely articulates the nature of thinking and decision-making that have been freely accepted by most CEOs, and, at various times, contrasts it to the thinking and decision-making freely accepted by the Lean CEOs. Compare-and-contrast is not equivalent to us-versus-them, nor does examining differences and similarities in methods constitute an ad hominem attack. While this is a serious study, hopefully you could find the humor as well as the diverse sympathies embedded in it.

9. In his book, *The Instinct of Workmanship* (Veblen, 1914), Veblen characterized the mismanagement of industry this way (p. 193):

> "If the 'efficiency engineers' are to be credited, it is probably within the mark to say that the net aggregate gains from industry fall short of what they might be by some fifty per cent, owing to the trained inability of the businessmen in control to appreciate and give effect to the visible

technological requirements of the industries from which they draw their gain. To appreciate the kind and degree of this commonplace mismanagement of industry it is only necessary to contrast the facility, circumspection, shrewd strategy and close economy shown by these same businessmen in the organization and management of their pecuniary, fiscal and monetary operations, as against the waste of time, labour and materials that abounds in the industries under their control."

(Not that the "efficiency engineers" of the early 20th century were the same as today's Lean consultants. They were a derivative commercial version of the people who created Scientific management, just as Lean consultants are derivative commercial versions of the people who created the Toyota production system. In the early 1900s, the "efficiency engineers" were seen by the creators and adherents of Scientific management as largely unqualified and opportunistic, in parallel with how many Lean consultants are viewed by the creators and adherents of TPS today).

Veblen continues (p. 222):

"It is the testimony of these efficiency engineers that relatively few pecuniary captains in command of industrial enterprises have a sufficient comprehension of the technological facts to understand and accept the findings of the technological experts who so argue for the

elimination of preventable wastes, even when the
issue is presented statistically in terms of price."

Thus, even when waste in presented in financial terms that
executives can easily understand, the executives still do not
understand the vast opportunities for the improvement that
exist in their operations. Veblen attributes this to the wide
separation between the management of the enterprise and
the management of industrial processes. He contrasts how
the top company managers in the earlier days of industry
were closer to the technologies of industrial processes than
the top company managers in his day due to the focus by
the latter on money as the singular measure of efficiency in
all processes and all transactions. Veblen said (p. 224):

> "That the business community is so permeated with
> incapacity and lack of insight in technological
> matters is doubtless due proximately to the fact that
> their attention is habitually directed to the pecuniary
> issue of industrial enterprise; but more
> fundamentally and unavoidably it is due to the large
> volume and intricate complications of the current
> technological scheme, which will not permit any
> man to become a competent specialist in an alien
> and exacting field of endeavour, such as business
> enterprise, and still acquire and maintain an
> effectual and working acquaintance with the state of
> the industrial arts."

The obvious solution to this problem – long known to the
creators and adherents of Lean and Lean consultants, the
creators and adherents of TPS, and the creators and

adherents of Scientific management and efficiency engineers before them – is to periodically engage top company leaders in improvement activities so that they may gain sufficient familiarity with industrial processes under their command, witness the vast waste and inefficiency first-hand, and contribute to their elimination. However, as has been previous explained in this chapter, a benefit of wealth is the power to control the corporate agenda to suit executives' predilections and thus eliminate or quarantine activities perceived to be of a low priority or simply nonsense in relation to executives' time and interests.

10. In a later work, Veblen (Veblen, 1921) provides an alternative yet complimentary explanation for executive resistance to Lean that, combined with executive culture and their pecuniary interests, adds much greater weight to the likely cause of the observed effect. Veblen attributed executive indifference to process improvements made by production engineers to the "layman" status of the "captains of finance." As the size and scope of industrial enterprises grew, executives' role focused increasingly on financial management of the enterprise, which, in turn, meant that they became increasingly disconnected from the industrial processes. At the same time, the industrial processes became more diversified and complex, requiring staff with greater engineering and technological capabilities. Over time, the industrial processes that produced profit and which provided executives with "free income" became incomprehensible to them, and hence their reduction to layman status. That, in turn, resulted in increased executive conservatism with respect to innovation, experimentation, and change. They were content to "let well enough alone."

Thus grew the division in focus and understanding between executives responsible for financial management of the enterprise and those responsible for management of industrial processes. Maintaining or expanding profits by lowering costs through process improvement was perceived by executives as high risk because they were unfamiliar with industrial processes. Other mechanisms, such as those shown in Table 1-2, CEOs Wealth Creation Playbook, were perceived as low risk and therefore more useful. The result of "disjointed one-eyed management" was an inability by executives to see or comprehend the "lag, leak, and friction" (waste, unevenness, and unreasonableness) contained in all industrial processes and which plagued the efficiency and effectiveness of the business throughout.

Veblen characterized the benefit that comes when production experts take over management of the enterprise (p. 68):

> "So that wherever the production experts are now taking over the management, out of the dead hand of the self-made captains, and wherever they have occasions to inquire into the established conditions of production, they find the ground cumbered with all sorts of incredible makeshifts of waste and inefficiency – such makeshifts as would perhaps pass muster with any moderately stupid elderly layman, but which look like blindfold guesswork to these men who know something of advanced technology and its working-out."

Veblen commented on the gain in productive output that is possible if management is left to the production experts (pp. 70-71).

> "And all the while it is an open secret that with a reasonably free hand the production experts would today readily increase the ordinary output of industry by several fold, – variously estimated at some 300 per cent. to 1200 per cent. of the current output. And what stands in the way of so increasing the ordinary output of goods and services is business as usual."

Veblen noted how production experts' presentation of the facts were ignored by top corporate managers (pp. 72-73):

> "During the opening yeas of the new [20th] century a lively interest centered on the views and expositions of these two groups of industrial experts [Scientific management experts and consulting engineers]; and not least was the interest aroused by their exhibits of current facts indicating an all-pervading lag, leak, and friction in the industrial system, due to its disjointed and one-eyed management..."

The logical and consequent result of Veblen's analysis is the outsourcing of non-core competencies by executives. Because the layman does not understand or care about the workings of industrial processes, they outsource it, creating an organization that is ever-more suited to the limited and diminishing capabilities of the layman. The   layman executive will become increasingly inexpert in future industrial processes as business becomes even more technologically oriented through digitization and digital transformation, resulting in a continuation of "business as usual" (Table 1-2).

Toyota's consistent success is attributable in large part to a long-standing commitment to the careful and conscientious management of industrial processes, enshrined in their management system, The Toyota Way, thus avoiding the layperson status that befalls the "one-eyed" (financial) managers, as well as avoiding the "lag, leak, and friction" that perpetually plagues business efficiency and effectiveness, to the detriment of all but the executive class.

11. For nearly 30 years, Lean movement leaders tried to make a business case for Lean, one that would appeal to the CEOs of large companies. The first 20 years focused almost exclusively of the technical methods of Lean, while the last 10 years has seen the addition of "Respect for People" and embrace of humans – especially workers. The business case for Lean failed to persuade the CEOs of large corporations. Going forward, the case for Lean will be made using a broader societal context (Womack, 2017b). However, it seems unlikely that executives raised on classical political economy would be interested in a new social approach that features stable employment, comfortable income, and fulfilling work. A rationale for corporations to adopt Lean based on jobs and societal welfare is likely to be even less appealing than the failed business case for Lean that was based on banishing waste. Grand visions of what is best for society (social engineering) are uniquely situational,

politically difficult, and quick to generate strong defensive routines among the people who have interests vested in wealth and power. On its face, the pivot to a social context for Lean seems more likely to be a strategy designed to keep Lean alive until such time when jobs and social welfare become appealing objectives to CEOs and their Boards. Lean proffered as a cure for society's ills could inadvertently hasten its demise. Scientific management was also proffered as a cure for society's ills, and is one of the primary reasons why it failed to gain traction in business and elsewhere.

12. Much of what has been said in this chapter is substantially true for the executives of smaller corporations as well as the owners of small family-owned businesses.

References

Ballé, M., Jones, D., Chaize, J., and Fiume, O. (2017), *The Lean Strategy: Using Lean to Create Competitive Advantage, Unleash Innovation, and Deliver Sustainable Growth*, McGraw Hill Education, New York, NY

Bryne, A. (2012), *The Lean Turnaround: How Business Leaders Use Lean Principles to Create Value and Transform Their Company*, McGraw Hill Education, New York, NY

Cook-Taylor, R.W. (1891), *The Modern Factory System*, Kegan Paul, Trench, Trübner, & Co., Ltd., London

Ingram, J.K. (1888), *A History of Political Economy*, MacMillan and Co., New York, NY

Jensen, M. and Meckling, W. (1976) "Theory of the Firm: Managerial Behavior, Agency Costs and Ownership Structure," *Journal of Financial Economics,* October, Vol. 3, No. 4, pp. 305-360

Krafcik, J.F. (1988), "Triumph of the Lean Production System," *Sloan Management Review*, Vol. 30, No. 1, pp. 41-52

Monden, Y. (1983), *Toyota Production System: Practical Approach to Production Management*, Engineering and Management Press, Norcross, Georgia

Morris-Suzuki, T. (1989), *A History of Japanese Economic Thought*, Routledge, London

Ohno, T. (1988), *Toyota Production System – Beyond Large-Scale Production*, Productivity Press, Portland, OR

Ohno, T. and Mito, S. (1988), *Just-In-Time For Today and Tomorrow*, Productivity Press, Cambridge, Mass., p. xii

Parker, A. and Rucker, P. (2017), "'Trump Betrays Everyone': The President Has a Long Record as an Unpredictable Ally," *The Washington Post*, 9 September, http://wapo.st/2gS6pzx?tid=ss_tw&utm_term=.618f35176 0c5, accessed 24 September 2017

Person, H. (Ed.) in Taylor, F.W. (1947), *Scientific Management: Comprising Shop Management, Principles of Scientific Management, Testimony Before the House Committee*, H. Person, Ed., Harper & Brothers Publishers, New York, NY, p. xii

Rother, M. (2009), *Toyota Kata: Managing People for Improvement, Adaptiveness and Superior Results*, McGraw-Hill Education, New York, NY

Rother, M. (2017), *The Toyota Kata Practice Guide: Practicing Scientific Thinking Skills for Superior Results in 20 Minutes a Day*, McGraw-Hill Education, New York, NY

Schein, E. (1996), "Three Cultures of Management: The Key to Organizational Learning," *Sloan Management Review*, Fall 1996, Vol. 38, No. 1, pp. 9-20

Taylor, F. W. (1911), *The Principles of Scientific Management*, Harper and Brothers, New York, NY

Veblen, T. (1899), *The Theory of the Leisure Class: An Economic Study of Institutions*, Macmillan Co., New York, NY

Veblen, T. (1904), *The Theory of Business Enterprise*, Charles Scribner's Sons, New York, NY

Veblen, T. (1914), *The Instinct of Workmanship: And the State of the Industrial Arts*, The Macmillan Company, New York, NY

Veblen, T. (1921), *The Engineers and the Price System*, B.W. Huebsch, Inc., New York, NY

Wayland, F. (1885), *The Elements of Political Economy*, recast by A. Chapin, Sheldon and Company, New York, NY

Womack, J., Jones, D., and Roos, D. (1990), *The Machine that Changed the World*, Rawson Associates, New York, NY

Womack, J. and Jones, D. (1996), *Lean Thinking: Banish Waste and Create Wealth in Your Corporation: The Story of Lean Production*, Simon & Schuster, New York, NY

Womack, J.P. (2017), "Jim Womack on Where Lean Has Failed and Why Not to Give Up," *Planet Lean: The Lean Global Network Journal*, 29 August, http://planet-lean.com/jim-womack-on-where-lean-has-failed-and-why-not-to-give-up, accessed 19 September 2017

Womack, J.P. (2017a), "Reflections on a Week in Toyota City," *Planet Lean: The Lean Global Network Journal*, 26 September, http://planet-lean.com/reflections-on-a-week-in-toyota-city, accessed 27 September 2017

Womack, J.P. (2017b), "Create Stable, Fulfilling Jobs to Fully Benefit from Lean," *Planet Lean: The Lean Global Network Journal*, 31 October, http://planet-lean.com/create-stable-fulfilling-jobs-to-fully-benefit-from-lean, accessed 31 October 2017

2

Political Economy, Politics, and Lean Management

Abstract

For more than 100 years, both the creators and devoted advocates of progressive management, beginning with early 20th century Scientific Management to late 20th century Lean management, have viewed the problem of gaining widespread acceptance among the leaders of large corporations as technocratic. Following the failure of decades-long technocratic approaches, the problem then becomes seen as behavioral, where changes in top executive leadership behaviors will result in acceptance of progressive management. This approach has also largely failed, and suggests a fundamental, consistent, and long-lived misunderstanding of the problem that one is trying to solve. Chapter 2 shows that acceptance for progressive Lean management among the leaders of large corporations is neither a technocratic nor a behavioral problem. Instead, it is a political problem. As such, the solution to acceptance of Lean management lies in the realm of political strategies and tactics. While this approach is both challenging and long-term in commitment, it offers a workable means to replace archaic classical management thinking and practice with modern Lean management thinking and practice in large corporations.

Note: This chapter explores the research question: Why does Lean management fail to take root in organizations?

Introduction

Beginning with early 20th century Scientific Management through late 20th century Lean management, innovative systems of management practice have struggled to gain widespread acceptance among the leaders of large corporations. While success rates have not been scientifically measured, evidence of successful transformation from classical to progressive management practice, as periodically reported in academic literature and trade press, is on the order of two to five percent.

Successful transformation is defined as fulfilling the human spirit and beneficial intents of progressive management coupled with the skilled technical application of the principles, methods, and tools as articulated in the writings of the creators of progressive management systems: Frederick Winslow Taylor for Scientific Management (Taylor, 1911) and James P. Womack and Daniel T. Jones for Lean management (Womack and Jones, 1996) (see Note 1). This definition implies long-term commitment to progressive management through the learning and application of new management principles and practices by all employees – including the executive team.

This raises the obvious question: Why has progressive Lean management been shunned by recent generations of executives despite its proven superiority in terms of business results and positive outcomes for stakeholders (employees, suppliers, customers, investors, and communities) and society at-large (Womack et al., 1990; Byrne, 2012)? There have been many attempts to answer this question – mostly guesses, which lie at a superficial level and are therefore deficient. Despite being deficient, these guesses inform sustained efforts and investments towards advancing Lean management and gaining its broader acceptance.

Chapter 1 probed beyond the superficial level to examine the distinctive culture and characteristics of the executive class. It showed that the fundamental basis for executive resistance to progressive management lies in the numerous interconnected details that comprise executive culture. Executives view Lean as antithetical or irrelevant to their class and cultural interests. Unaware of this near-impenetrable cultural barrier, the creators of progressive management and their devoted advocates assumed that executives would embrace the new management system though the combined presentation of data, facts, and logical arguments, and by showcasing actual companies that have attained success. These methods of persuasion proved to be largely ineffective, much to the frustration of those seeking to advance progressive management.

To put it succinctly, adopting Lean management requires executives to reverse long-honored traditions and quickly discard entrenched habits of thought that have consistently yielded favorable business results as well as notoriety and wealth. When carefully studied, we find that executive culture is far more complex and intertwined than is apparent to the casual observer. We also find that executives are unwilling to voluntarily reveal the honored traditions and habits of thought that create resistance to Lean management. So, these must be recognized and categorized by inductive reasoning, and then verified or substantiated through deductive reasoning.

It is now clear that the problem of executive acceptance of Lean has long been misunderstood. It is also clear why the methods long used to gain acceptance have repeatedly failed, and why doing more of the same (Womack, 2017) will not work. The problem must be re-framed and seen in a different context, and different methods must be used to expand the practice of Lean management in large corporations.

This chapter extends the previous chapter by framing the acceptance of progressive Lean management in a new way, as a political problem, rather than as the technocratic (use of the science and engineering methods to solve socio-economic problems) and behavioral (psychological and leadership) problems that it has long been thought to be. When seen from this perspective, new avenues for influencing executives to accept Lean management become available to those whose work it is to sell or promote Lean. In some cases, resolution of political problems can be quick. The usual case, however, is that political problems require lengthy and highly coordinated campaigns to resolve conflicting interests. However, any successful political campaign is subject to reversal over time by competing interests. So, while the direction is clear, permanency in any outcome is unlikely.

As a political problem, Lean management has embedded within it a complex combination of economic, social, and historical factors (Emiliani, 2011) that must be unraveled to a degree that can inform and initiate tangible actions directed towards achieving broad-based acceptance. In the past, these economic, social, and historical factors have been largely ignored by the leaders of the Lean community. If this continues in the future, then Lean management is destined to go the way of Scientific Management (Person, 1947). It will fade from existence, and a subset of its technical methods and tools will be subsumed into classical management practice. If this outcome is to be avoided, the economic, social, and historical factors that animate the political problem can no longer be ignored.

We begin by examining fundamental elements of 19th century classical political economy, which forms the root basis for understanding the function of business in economic terms. Executives are deeply influenced by classical political economy and its evolutionary narrowing to neoclassical economics. Therefore, one must understand classical political economy to understand the economic perspective of executives both past and present. This, along with executive culture, is heavily intertwined with social and historical factors that must be understood to affect political change.

Next comes a Veblenesque exposition of political power and influence exercised by the executive class over the worker class to ensure perpetuation of its vested rights and interests (Veblen, 1899, 1904, 1914, 1921; Teggart, 1932; Plotkin and Tilman, 2011). This perspective provides a more comprehensive understanding of the relationship between executive power and privilege and subordination of the working class to satisfy the political interests of the executive class. It also illuminates the chasm between classical management and Lean management practice in relation to political values and sentiments. These political values and sentiments are shown to be dramatically different between executives who practice classical management and those who practice progressive Lean management.

A way forward is proposed for gaining broader acceptance of progressive Lean management using political strategies and tactics that have long been proven to be effective in other settings. With this as a baseline method for political change, it is expected that those wishing to advance Lean management will be inspired to think of novel and lower-cost means of effecting political change, put their ideas into practice, and then identify gaps between their plan and actual results, which will initiate Plan-Do-Check-Act cycles and result in improved political effectiveness over time.

Finally, nothing written in this chapter should be construed as derogation of executives, nor does it have anything to do with their intelligence or commitment, as all executives are intelligent, educated, and committed people. Rather, the conflicts in political values and sentiments are merely the result of inherited habits of mind and cognitive biases to which all humans are susceptible, combined with predilections for power, wealth, and influence, and changes in societal views of moral rectitude and virtue in business and economics. This chapter is merely an elucidation of the human political, economic, and social condition in the context of business.

Classical Political Economy

What is classical political economy in relation to the function of business interests (versus the state or the overall economy)? Let's begin by reviewing some key concepts of classical political economy as it was understood in the mid- to late-1800s. Then, we will examine what has happened since then because of changes in focus or interpretation these key concepts of classical political economy.

What follows is a basic outline of several key concepts of classical political economy that are relevant to this chapter. The source of the quoted text that follows is the 1885 edition of Francis Wayland's book, *The Elements of Political Economy*, edited by Aaron Chapin after Wayland's passing (Wayland, 1885). This widely praised and influential book, used to educate countless students, remained in-print for nearly half a century (see Note 2). Political economy emanated from British and French scholars of the 18th and 19th centuries. Though it is pre-scientific (philosophical) in form, it proved to be very influential among businessmen around the world, and to this day.

What is "political economy?" The word "political" is derived from the Greek word "polis," which means community, public, city, or state (not "politics" in the sense of electoral politics). The word "economy" comes from the Greek word "economia," which means household law or administration (of allocations or distributions). Therefore, the term "political economy" has the approximate literal meaning of: Rules or laws of distribution within a community.

Political economy is an expansive topic covering subjects such as labor, capital, consumption, production, distribution, exchange, banking currency, free trade, and protectionism. For the purposes of this chapter, we will focus on definitions, fundamental laws, labor, and capital. Wayland defines political economy as (italics and bold font appear in the original publication of *The Elements of Political Economy*):

> "*...that branch of Social Science which treats of the production and application of wealth to the well-being of men in society*" (p. 4).

Political economy is based on four fundamental laws (pp. 4-6):

1. God has made man *a creature of desires* and constituted the material world in which he lives with qualities and powers available for the *gratification of those desires... There is no assignable limit to the development of either men's desires or nature's resources.*

2. For desires above the very simplest wants of the animal, *man must, by Labor, force nature to yield her hidden resources.*

3. *The exertion of labor establishes a right of* **Property** *in the fruits of labor*, and the idea of *exclusive possession* is a necessary consequence.

4. *With the right of property, comes also the possibility and the right of* **Exchange**, or the mutual transfer of possessions between man and man, and

between different communities and countries. One
may do what he will with his own.

Wayland describes the "motive to effort" as follows (p. 6):

"Political economy regards *self-interest* as a universal
motive of human action… It assumes labor is
irksome, and that every body [sic] desires the utmost
gratification with the least possible exertion."

Two structural problems in political economy are
immediately recognizable. The first is the community or
public basis of political economy and, simultaneously,
adoration of individual self-interest – thus discounting the
social and community bonds that historically define
humanity and its quest for survival. A secondary assumption
is that self-interest is beneficial to the community at-large.
At face value, and in practice, the two are typically in
conflict with one another, as self-interest can undercut
cooperation, with self-interest often winning over the
interests of the community. In business, this manifests itself
as large gains for owners (often as passive or absentee
shareholders) that greatly exceed the gains realized by those
who perform work. In recent decades, the disparity has
become greatly enlarged, making it very difficult for labor to
gratify their desires.

The second structural problem in political economy is the
view that work is "irksome." This pessimistic assumption
about humanity means that people are lazy, unintelligent,
and irresponsible (Theory X of human motivation;
McGregor, 1960). This view of humanity has unlimited

potential and kinetic political utility. It conforms to the needs of those who desire power, wealth, and status through the appropriation of other's labors (Veblen, 1899, 1914), and is fundamental to the thinking behind classical management. The view of work as "irksome" contradicts the difficult work spontaneously taken by human beings in prehistoric times to assure survival of the species (Veblen, 1899, 1914). Rather than an assumption, the fact is that human beings are not fundamentally lazy, unintelligent, or irresponsible (Theory Y of human motivation; McGregor, 1960). Lean management recognizes people as hard-working, intelligent, and responsible.

In the chapter on division of labor, Wayland says (p. 50):

> "The largest and best results with the least
> expenditure of labor are desired."

This is a point of agreement between classical and Lean management with respect to labor (though not on "largest" or "best"), though the thinking, methods, and outcomes are different. In classical management, there is a reflexive desire to replace people with expensive machines and quickly cast workers aside. Sudden loss of employment is an expression of executive power and coercion over workers. In Lean management, action is preceded by careful analysis to determine what machines and people can do or not do best, either separately or together. People are not cast aside if they are replaced by machines; they are re-deployed to other work areas. This is an expression of executive perception and confidence in worker's ability to think.

Furthermore, in Lean management, executives abide by a related dictum, which is foreign to classical management:

> Favorable results with the least expenditure
> of capital equipment are desired.

As capital equipment, and the space necessary to house it, can form a large part of fixed costs – which impinges upon both profitability and competitiveness – Lean management seeks to minimize all direct and indirect costs associated with capital equipment by utilizing the least expensive equipment capable of performing the necessary function. If possible, the equipment is so inexpensive that it is expensed as if it were a consumable item (e.g. buy a $300 mini drill press instead of $10,000 drill press, or use ten $5 hand clamps instead of a $7,000 durable tooling fixture that one must pay annual taxes on). The difference is profound. It is the difference between how executives view workers: replace people with machines whenever possible because workers are lazy, unintelligent, and irresponsible (classical management, Theory X), or, use machines where appropriate and retain worker because they are hard-working, intelligent, and responsible (Lean management, Theory Y) (Goodman, 2017).

In the chapter on cooperation between labor and capital, Wayland offers stern warnings against capital taking advantage of labor, and vice versa:

> **"The true relation of Labor and Capital is that of Partners, Co-adjutors** *for a common end,* – **Sharers** *in a joint result...* In the production of

wealth, each is necessary to the other; each is helpless without the other. Antagonism between the representatives of these two essentials to the increase of wealth is unnatural and ruinous to the interests of both." (p. 88)

"The common sense of men... most fully recognizes labor and capital as *the two necessary and inseparable factors* in the production of wealth. It is pitiable to see how often minds are sophisticated by some sort of false philosophy so as to lose their *common sense* with respect to these things... Abstractly considered, labor and capital stand toward each other on an *Equality*. If there is any difference, capital is the more helpless of the two. For it is nothing but dead matter, whereas labor is a vital force..." (p. 89)

"The happy co-operation of labor and capital depends on the certainty that each shall have its just reward. Nobody questions the right of the laborer to the fruit of his toil... The right of capital to its reward... stands on the same basis of intrinsic justice." (p. 96)

"Nothing else so disables industry and hinders the growth of wealth as the selfish greed which would rob either partner of his reward or make it insecure." (p. 97)

"...it is of the highest importance that both parties [capital and labor] as they meet should be capable of

> taking broad views of their common interests and
> mutual dependence... there is on one side [capital],
> some temptation to take advantage of the superior
> knowledge, in a way to wrong the weak and
> dependent; and on the other side [labor], there is a
> tendency... to chafe and complain and make
> unreasonable demands... Harmony between the
> two requires *mutual respect*, and the basis of this
> mutual respect is *self-respect* on the part of each...
> (pp. 107-108)

Wayland was clear that political economy must serve a range of human interests in proprietous ways. He cautioned capitalists in their predatory hunt for wealth and recognized the great risk posed by excessive self-interest, which would lead to calamity.

> "Intellectual cultivation may exist without
> promoting rectitude and virtue. In this case,
> however, its only effect is to stimulate desire,
> unbalanced by the love of right, until the mad
> passions of men break down the very structure of
> society and self-interest reduced to pure *selfishness*,
> destroys mutual confidence and cooperation, and
> reigns supreme in anarchy, fatal alike to the
> production and enjoyment of wealth." (pp. 108-
> 109)

This is a warning to businessmen against succumbing to a false or defective logic that would justify "mad passions" towards increasing one's wealth at the expense of other human beings and the community. Rectitude and virtue, and concern for fellow man, are indispensable elements to the pursuit of wealth and to avoid wrecking one's own business. In recent decades, it has been plain to see the reckless pursuit of wealth and business bankruptcies fueled by debt piled onto corporations by financiers.

In sum, these passages reveal the human side of political economy. Economics, as a social science, must respect humans and their varied interests, regardless of class, and not focus solely on pecuniary interests – particularly among those who have the advantage of power and wealth. Executives of classical management organizations who decide to adopt Lean management invariably leave out the human side of Lean; what is known as "Respect for People." This is more by design than by chance, as "Respect for People" implies the necessity for leaders to empower people in the working class, and which therefore translates into loss of control over one's dominion, both in the present, and, more dangerously, in the future. The whole of executive function is therefore unacceptably compromised by these three simple words: "Respect for People." This, alone, is a deal-breaker for the adoption of Lean management in its full form (see Note 3), though it does not preclude executives from demanding that workers use selected Lean methods and tools in the performance of their work.

It is obvious that since Wayland's time, political economy evolved into a more mechanistic (i.e. less humanistic) understanding and practice among capitalists that support their narrow pecuniary interests, and to extend and legitimize their power over the working classes. The elements of political economy that were challenging or difficult to put into practice – humanity, fairness, justice, cooperation, etc. – were diminished or ignored over time in favor of expediency to yield the preferred outcomes sought by the capitalists. The evolution of political economy into neoclassical economics cumulatively carries forward the primary elements that best satisfy predilections for power and dominance over the lower classes. In other words, the surviving elements of political economy fully supports the predatory interests and needs of capital over labor. Today's business economics is a reflection of the dominant interests of the chieftains, kings, and queens of long ago – political power, war, and wealth (the prize). War and warlike habits or impulses are commonly found in business - e.g. hostile takeovers, conflict with suppliers, mass layoffs, union-busting, etc. The conquest of other companies, organizations, groups, or people are rooted in politics and represents the highest honor that one can attain in business. As such, business is first and foremost a political institution.

Despite the long and continuing diminishment of workers interests with respect to wages and benefits (reductions in the "just reward"), and workers' concomitant ongoing dissatisfaction ("chafe and complain"), the executive class and the corporations they represent enjoy strong loyalties among workers – though surely not their best work. Perhaps counterintuitively, the forced removal of the humanistic elements of political economy has strengthened the validity of economics as a source of influence in business affairs because workers assume management knows best, they fear confronting the powerful, and they possess no mechanism for executive accountability. In classical management, capital is more-or-less free to appropriate labor's "just reward" anytime it desires. In Lean management, capital and labor seek a more harmonious balance, as they take, in Wayland's words, "broad views of their common interests and mutual dependence."

Politics

A problem is political when there are conflicting interests among various classes of people or stakeholders. Lean management produces myriad economic, social, and historical problems, and exposes deep conflicts with those who are vested in classical management. These conflicting interests clearly reveal the advancement of Lean management to be a political problem at its core. This does not discount the technocratic and behavioral problems associated with Lean management that were identified many decades ago. Rather, it casts the problem of acceptance of Lean management by executives in new light which, if solved, may allow the solutions to the technical and behavioral problems developed previously to flourish.

The fundamental purpose of politics is to exert control over people to compel them to do things that they would not otherwise choose to do. To exert control in business, executives must possess power, or be recognized by others as possessing power that can be exercised over them. Economics must rely on political power to achieve its objectives, thus requiring executive preoccupation to span both domains. This includes power and prestige as seen internally and especially by external organizations and competitors. The political nature of organizations is evident in part by management decision-making, which invariably favors executives' interests over the interests of employees and suppliers, and often even customers and passive investors (stockholders) as well. Evidence for this exists primarily within the bounds of illogical thinking; i.e. false yet plausible-sounding theories and arguments that support the desired political and economic outcomes; e.g. "management's primary responsibility is to maximize shareholder value" (Bower and Paine, 2017). In this way, political power is claimed ahead of human life and the basic necessities for human existence (Veblen, 1899, 1914).

Power-seeking and conflict-making are the *sine qua non* of politics. As circumstances and events change from day to day, corporate political power and conflict help assure that the institution of business remains bound to the past. This enduring connection largely extinguishes attempts to bring management practice forward into the present day and help assure that the business is adaptable to future changes. Additionally, power-seeking and conflict-making distort objectivity and dampen executive curiosity, which blinds executives to the true condition of the company and each process within it. The perniciousness of political power manifests itself in the inability for employees to speak truth to power, thereby weakening the human (social) foundation upon which business rests. Persistently operating human systems on the basis of irrationality has consequences.

Despite being antiquated by the standards of current-day science and technology, business as an institution and classical management as its animating method, are idolized, thereby lending approval to archaic traits that do not serve, or poorly serve, human interests. Within this frame, any effort to renovate, reform, or transform classical management is viewed with great skepticism and distrust. Radical or revolutionary change in established beliefs and practices are seen as subversive and therefore instinctively unwelcome, resulting in the enormous staying-power of classical management. This helps explain why Lean success stories are seen by most executives as unconvincing, and, by extension, why the methods and tactics used to promote Lean over the last 30 years have proven to be largely unsuccessful. In short, the human and technical rationality of Lean, rooted in engineering mindset and practice (Taylor, 1911; Ohno, 1988; Woollard and Emiliani, 2009), has failed to weaken classical management's grip on executive function.

The political features of classical management consist of tangible and spiritual relics of the long-ago past; values and habits that have been dutifully carried forward by agents of capital for the purpose of preserving power and privilege. In other words, antiquated ideas continue to inhabit modern brains. As such, the political features are entrenched and not easily altered or removed. A useful analogy may be as follows: Newton's first law of motion is popularly stated as: An object in motion will remain in motion (at constant velocity and direction) unless it is acted on by a net non-zero force. The "object" in this case is the class of powerful and wealthy people who seek to perpetuate their interests (represented by "velocity") by assuring that the interests of other classes ("net non-zero forces") do not act or impinge upon them. This is the first law of executive power.

To avoid "net non-zero forces" from acting upon them, executives have to put into place and faithfully uphold certain political traditions and practices that position corporate power ahead of improving the human condition in the workplace and, by extension, to the homelife and society overall. Many of the political traditions and practices amount to continuous harassment of the weak (workers) by the powerful. Harassment is used as a tool to visibly display exercises of power and maintain control, driven by a lack of empathy, acceptance of class distinctions, and the need to dominate others. Putting workers "in their place" is but one of a large collection of honorific acts that executives actively seek in fulfillment of their perceived purpose.

In Lean management, executives are far less troubled by "net non-zero forces" emanating from workers, or other stakeholders such as suppliers, customers, investors, and communities. In fact, such "net non-zero forces" are welcomed because they represent opportunities for improvement – whether it is improved human relations, lower cost, better quality, shorter lead-times, and so on – and to build capabilities in employees that accrue towards improving the competitive strength of the company. The Lean executive's measure of control is whether workers are recognizing and quickly (and creatively) correcting problems, and whether they are learning from their experiences and applying those learnings to new problems that they will encounter in the future.

Successful Lean management balances authority and resistance, where resistance manifests itself as a sanctioned form of serviceable insubordination – Toyota-style kaizen –

a rebellious habit among workers to think for themselves, rather than simply accept management's dictate on how best to perform the work. Kaizen imbues workers with self-respect, liberty to think, and self-directed ideation and execution. Lean executives give their hearty approval to be challenged in this manner, as it has proven to be responsive to the fundamental short- and long-term needs of a business and its customers: lower costs, shorter lead-times, and higher quality and productivity. Kaizen, a controlled anarchic process, is seen as preferable to uncontrolled hidden worker resentments that generate widespread passive-aggressive behaviors. This contrasts with classical management, in which workers who desire to think are forced to accept "do what you are told" directives, reflecting the coercive power of executive authority and the passivity of workers whose quiescence is taken as accredited evidence of successful leadership.

The political traditions and practices in organizations that practice classical management are vastly different from Lean management organizations, and provide an indication of how difficult it is for executives to adopt Lean management in its full form. Political traditions and practices become stable political values and sentiments that carry over from one generation to the next. Fundamentally, Lean does not offer compelling reasons for top executives to abandon the political values and sentiments long associated with classical management. Table 2-1 compares several political values and sentiments of classical management and Lean management, and includes some shared values and sentiments as well.

Table 2-1: Comparison of Some Political Values and Sentiments

Classical Management	Lean Management	Shared (similar but not identical views)
Tradition	Reform	Freedom
Authority	Egalitarianism	Competition
Hierarchy	De-classification	Free Markets
Loyal	Competent	Self-Reliance
Bureaucracy	De-centralized	Opportunity
Self-Interest	Shared Responsibility	Individual Resourcefulness
Problems are Bad	Problems are Good	Family
Rationalism	Empiricism (Scientific Method)	Apprehensive of Government
Spirituality	Corporeal	
Laissez-Faire (let it be)	Improvement (take action)	
Distrust	Mutual Trust	
Aggressive	Diplomatic	
Gain at Expense of Others	Mutual Prosperity	
Labor as Expense	Labor as Assets	
Strict	Nurturing	
Defend Existing Order	Fairness	
Status-Quo (indifference)	Evolution (curiosity)	

* Many business outcomes are also shared such as profits, growth, market share, etc. However, the methods used for achieving these business outcomes will be considerably different.

As is evident from Table 2-1, there are large differences in political values and sentiments between classical management and Lean management (see Note 4). It shows that the heart of the problem is a political problem – one of conflicting interests that can only be resolved through political, rather than technocratic or behavioral, solutions.

Table 2-1 also reveals why classical management survives despite the existence of a better management system (Lean), and why the existence of Lean management is often temporary and replaced by classical management when changes in leaders or company owners occur. Classical management:

- Reinforces class distinctions between executives and workers
- Supports aggressive and coercive interests of those in power
- Helps bind, coordinate, and perpetuate institutional control
- Valorizes executive power and prestige

In short, classical management is more useful to executives because it serves business leader's corporate political interests far better than Lean management (see Note 5). It reflects an archaic, prehistorical legacy of leaders' intellectual, spiritual, and methodological preferences for authority and control of over people in their personal struggle to survive internal and external conflict (Veblen, 1899; Teggart, 1932; Plotkin and Tilman, 2011) – rivalries and competition in the context of business. Said another way, anything that subverts subordination of the workforce is overtly or covertly cast aside by the executive class. Executives favoring classical management see Lean management as rife with practices that subvert workforce subordination and has the potential to result in anarchy.

Lean management presents an untenable political problem to executives that they clearly recognize and seek to avoid. Therefore, in most organizations where Lean exists, it amounts to little more than a façade.

Related to the politics of classical management is the interesting phenomenon of "Lean denial." Despite extensive evidence, most executives simply do not believe such remarkable business results can be achieved by adopting Lean management and associated leadership routines. Studies of other "denial" phenomena indicate that Lean is denied because of adherence to the political ideology of classical management, acceptance of authoritarian leadership (social dominance), preference for the status quo, lack of empathy for workers (and other stakeholders such as, suppliers, customers, investors, and communities), and desire to avoid new experiences or negative emotions. Each of these features are reflected in Table 2-1. This also explains why executives challenge Lean advocates to produce ever-more evidence proving that Lean management works, and why producing ever-more evidence is a fruitless effort. It is noteworthy that the first 30 years of Lean management has produced approximately ten times more books than the first 30 years of Scientific Management. Adherence to classical management political ideology appears to strengthen the more it is shown to be deficient. This suggests the need for a different approach for gaining more widespread acceptance of Lean management.

Table 2-1 also shows that there are also some important shared political values and sentiments that can be used to help bridge the large gaps between how executives think and what executives do in classical and Lean management. Often, one finds that there are more similarities than differences, and that differences tend to be magnified to an extent that they overshadow the similarities. Yet, Table 2-1 shows that this is not the case; the similarities are few (and, in the detail, not exactly the same, creating more areas of disagreement) and the differences are both many and significant. The way forward must take this into account (see Note 6).

There are also some remarkable gaps between what classical management leaders say they desire in employees who aspire to leadership roles, and how the executives in power typically conduct themselves. Table 2-2 illustrates the gaps. An effort is made to appear to desire progressive leadership characteristics (which happen to be closely aligned to Lean management), yet actual executive conduct is delimited by the political values and sentiments shown in Table 2-1.

Table 2-2: Qualities of Classical Management Leadership

Desired*	Actual
Empowerment	No
Engagement	No
Influence	Power
Innovation	Status Quo
Communication	As-Needed
Problem-Solving	Delegate
Transparency	No
Adaptability	No
Empathy	No
Continuous Learning	No

* (Barry, 2017)

Any young leader who has faced this contradiction knows they must make a choice. Those who chose to align with the desired qualities will likely be sidelined or seek employment elsewhere, while those who align with the actual qualities are far more likely to be promoted into senior positions. In essence, the gap between desired and actual functions as a useful ritualistic tool used by executives in power to assure that the next generation of executives is committed to classical management political values and sentiments, and that they recognize their duties and obligations to carry them forward. This assures that stakeholder conflict remains a permanent normalized feature of business strategy, tactics, and day-to-day management. It is only within a political context that the logic of perpetual, disrespectful (zero-sum) conflict could be construed as a useful thing of value. In Lean, stakeholder conflict is considered to be an abnormal condition.

A Way Forward

From the late 1980s through the mid-2000s, the work of Womack et al. (Krafcik, 1988; Womack et al. 1990; Womack and Jones, 1996) experienced tremendous success in gaining *interest* in Lean management (known as "lean production" until 2007) among executives, but little success in gaining *acceptance* (see Note 7). Overall, executive acceptance of Lean management has been limited, despite their continued demand that workers apply selected Lean methods and tools to their work to help reduce cost, lead-time, and defects – often in the form of a corporate "operating system" which contains only selected elements of Lean management practice (i.e. the previously mentioned façade).

It seems that the creators of Lean and their devoted advocates expected quick results from using the technocratic approach of presenting data, facts, logical arguments, and by profiling companies that had attained significant measures of success. This turns out to have been a significant miscalculation, one that mirrors the methods used in the 1910s through the 1930s to gain executive acceptance of Scientific Management. Neither achieved success beyond a handful of companies led by CEOs willing to learn new ways of doing things and challenge the status-quo. These same companies and their leaders became the customary lineup of speakers at conferences year-after-year. The behavioral approaches used in the last twenty years have also been unsuccessful in persuading the CEOs of large corporations to accept Lean management.

Failing to learn from the past has put Lean at a disadvantage during its first 30 years of existence. But what about the next 30 years? The way forward proposed by Womack (Womack 2017a) is to make the case for Lean based on a broader societal context – i.e., how Lean benefits society at-large. This admirable vision is described by Womack as follows (Womack 2017a):

> **"...it's not enough to deploy lean practices across their organizations and to promise not to lay off any employee due to kaizen. It's also necessary to create reciprocal obligations with employees and employment stability for the long run in order for lean methods to achieve their potential.** I can't hope to change senior managers' minds instantly about the feasibility of

creating this virtuous circle, but if we all engage in similar conversations over time perhaps we can." (bold in original)

In the last sentence, Womack hints at the necessity for a loosely coordinated political movement that will influence executives to accept Lean management. Womack continues:

"Creating stable lean enterprises provides several benefits for society more broadly... the great anxiety in the world today is jobs and fulfilling work. So, what we really need to focus on now is what I call 'social heijunka.' That means leveling the turbulence in society by making sure people have stable jobs, good jobs that provide for a comfortable living, and jobs with fulfilling work. And I think that is what the lean business system with the robust stabilization mechanisms inspired by Toyota's example can provide."

Womack proposes transforming the classical "business system" with a "lean business system" that offers continuing reciprocal benefits to both employer and employee, and hence society at-large.

"A key need, obviously, is to continually increase the value each employee is able to create, so that stable, well-paid and fulfilling jobs are feasible... focusing on this task – creating better and more secure jobs for everyone by improving the work of every worker and the systems that stabilize those jobs – puts our message in a broader social context. We will be talking about what's good for society, not just what's good for individual businesses and their owners. As we look ahead to the next phase of the Lean Movement, I think this is the key to our being relevant and exciting..."

Perhaps so, but the political problem – for both executives and workers – must be solved before the societal benefits can be realized. Therefore, as Lean is a political problem, one that affects much of the public (polity), political strategies and tactics are required (versus a Lean business strategy, *a la* Byrne 2015 and Ballé et al., 2017) and must be put into daily practice by a coalition of stakeholders committed to advancing Lean management and achieving more balance of business outcomes.

Political solutions often begin with donations from wealthy patrons to fund foundations, think tanks, academic research, grass-roots organizing, messaging across all forms of media, expansion of fundraising, and so on. Executives vested in classical management are not likely to fund a political movement that advances Lean management. A possible source of funds are the successful Lean leaders – those who have become wealthy due to Lean management that was practiced in the companies they led. However, successful Lean leaders have in the past shown little interest in funding efforts to expand or perpetuate Lean management. In addition, they are relatively few in number, thus limiting the extent and duration of financial support. Their heirs would have to be cultivated.

Another reason successful Lean leaders are unlikely to work towards delegitimizing classical management is because their wealthy peers still depend on it. It would require successful Lean leaders to criticize their business partners and friends, either directly or by proxy. Therefore, it seems they are unlikely to provide the funds necessary to advance a political solution to the problem of the acceptance of Lean by executives in large corporations. Even if they did, the funding needed for political action may be insufficient.

Yet, if these obstacles can be overcome, then a way forward is reasonably clear. Solutions to political problems typically follow a well-worn path that may prove to be helpful in the advancement of Lean management. Namely, create a populist movement whose focus is to bring modern progressive management practice into the world's corporations, both large and small.

Figure 2-1a illustrates the current political problem, which is a lack of interest in Lean management among both executives and workers, and long-standing acceptance (to greater or lesser extents) of Lean among the professional (salaried) class of workers. Figure 2-1b illustrates the potential political solution, which is to increase acceptance for Lean management among workers, which should, in turn, put pressure on executives to accept Lean management.

The fact that most organizations presently have a façade of Lean allows executives to expand adoption of Lean into its full form as a comprehensive system of management, thereby replacing classical management, without losing face.

This is a critically important political narrative because executives can rightfully claim they have long been interested or in favor of Lean management.

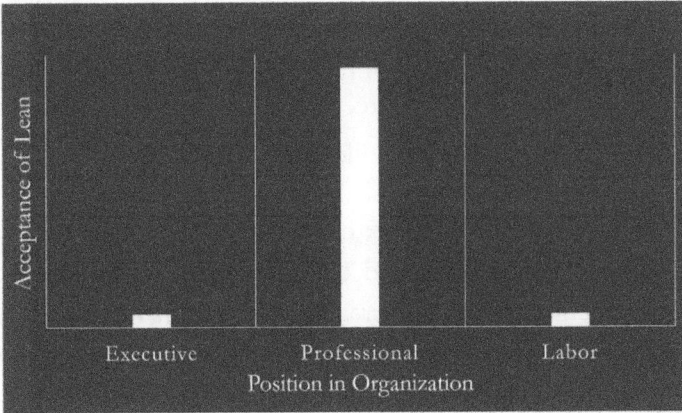

Figure 2-1a. Acceptance for Lean management has been greatest among professionals and weakest among executives and workers.

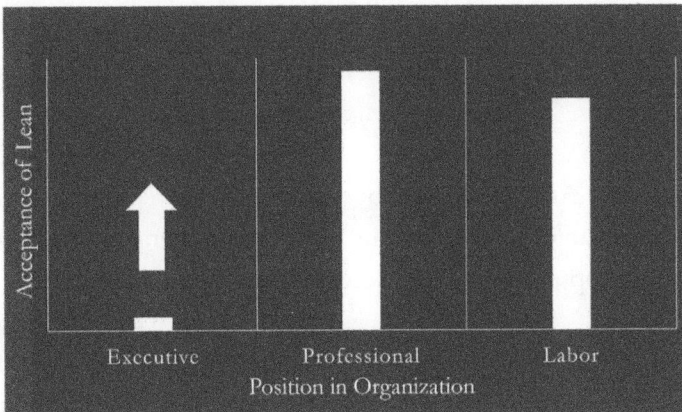

Figure 2-1b. Acceptance for Lean management among both workers and professional staff will put pressure on executives to accept Lean management in its full form.

It allows executives to evolve, in a measured and responsible way, enhancing and expanding executive status, to improve both corporate performance and economic fairness for workers (their "just reward" instead of wage stagnation) by reducing costs (thereby increasing profit margins and stock price for shareholders) through more effective use of resources: money, time, material, equipment, space, energy, employees, suppliers, etc.

A way forward is as follows: First, energize the large base of workers by discrediting and delegitimizing archaic classical management through the creation of alternative narratives, slogans, and imagery (pictures, symbols, etc.). This requires long-term and consistent advancement of compelling causal stories that working people will form strong emotional connections to (Stone, 1989). Quasi-fictional but credible anecdotes about workers and families made weary and impoverished, both mentally and financially, by classical management practice will be required. By their very nature, alternate political narratives must distort, misrepresent, or disregard knowledge (e.g. facts, expert opinions, professional judgments, etc.) and instead activate people's emotions. And there must be a continuous stream of potent and relatable talking points for public consumption to sustain populist energy and create a new national interest.

This mild prevarication is contradictory to the Lean mindset, as Lean is rooted in facts, data, reality, and hence the advancement of logical and rational arguments (see Note 8). This will require Lean, currently the domain of expert technocrats, to be turned over to boots-on-the-ground activists who can do what expert technocrats have been unable to do by meeting in secret and organizing conferences attended by like-minded people – influence the large class of working people, many of whom have never heard of Lean management. There needs to be a transition from Lean management holding the attention of a niche community of followers to gaining widespread popular attention.

Lean, expressed as a problem statement for executive consumption, can be summarized as follows (Womack and Jones, 1996):

- Who – Companies are not Lean
- What – Dissatisfied customers
- When – Ubiquitous; every process, every time, every day
- Where – Waste in value-creating business processes
- Why – Create wealth
- How – Lean transformation

This is a technocratic problem statement, one that recognized business too narrowly as an economic institution, and which resulted in a technocratic policy solution that dictated the types of people, efforts, and investments used to advance Lean management (i.e. data, facts, logical arguments, and profiling successful companies). However, the technocratic problem statement is of the naming-and-blaming variety and is given in a way that executives do not recognize as being a problem. In other words, the bad condition that is being expressed by the technocrats is not being heard. Nor is it understood by executives as a problem that can be placed under effective human control (Veblen, 1921, pp. 42-43). The intellectual argument does not resonate because causation is not seen as deterministic, it assigns accountability to executives, it places the burden of improvement on executives, and it asks executives to entrust technocrats with reform and thus disrupts their unitary right and freedom to exercise their power. Together, these result in emotional resistance and thus, rejection of Lean management by executives (see Note 6 and 9). The obvious solution is to change the emotional response from negative to positive.

To overcome emotional resistance, the drab, difficult-to-understand, unemotional language of Lean (e.g. gemba, muda) and imagery of Lean (e.g. value stream maps) may have to be re-cast in terms that are both more easily understandable and which embody characteristics that generate emotional acceptance among executives as a precursor to intellectual acceptance. Table 2-3 shows a future representation of Lean management in emotional terms that also provide a sense of safety and survival.

Table 2-3: Intellectual vs. Emotional Appeal of Lean

Current Intellectual Representation	Future Emotional Representation
Lean Management	Continuous Growth
Specify Value Identify the Value Stream Flow Pull Perfection	Steady Innovation
Continuous Improvement	Measurable Improvement
Respect for People	Employee Development

The future representation embodies emotional characteristics that could strongly appeal to executives because they:

- Like growth
- Like stability and keeping up with the competition (see Note 10)
- Like things that are measurable
- Think employees need development

These future representations should appeal to executive's sense of honor and may soften the rigid political ideology of classical management, characterized by acceptance of authoritarian leadership (social dominance), preference for the status quo, lack of empathy for workers (and other stakeholders such as, suppliers, customers, investors, and communities), and desire to avoid new experiences or negative emotions (Table 2-1). The future representations shown in Table 2-3 gives the sense that the problem of corporate performance can be placed under effective human control, in ways that are safe and do not risk one's career or which might create corporate anarchy.

The future representation also suggests a different problem statement, one that executives may feel they have more control over:

- Who – Elevate corporate performance
- What – Increase customer satisfaction
- When – Daily and weekly
- Where – Business processes

- Why – Grow sales
- How – Improve execution

This new problem statement has more the sentiment of a "business proposition." It recognizes business as a political institution and suggests a different policy solution and that different types of people, effort, and investment should be used to advance Lean management. The problem statement gives the impression of smaller, more manageable changes to the existing order than the earlier Lean problem statement (where "everything must change"; Byrne, 2012), to lessen the burden of reform on executives and distribute responsibility across all members of the organization. It is more likely to be adopted by decision-makers.

Additional tactics may be necessary to reiterate safety and survival. For example, the scary imagery of taking a "Lean leap" into the unknown (or "leap of faith") should be replaced with safer imagery. In addition, the successful Lean CEOs should speak explicitly about safety, as well as a few simple ways that classical management executives can prepare themselves for a safe and enjoyable Lean experience (rather than the ambiguous and puzzling "Lean journey"). Instead of emphasizing what executives must give up or lose, it will be advantageous to characterize what executives gain in terms of honor, influence, reputation, respect, and wealth – assuming they also care about the future and long-term benefits – and do not view the challenge they face as futile. It may also be helpful to get several dozen or, perhaps better yet, hundreds of executives to earnestly endorse Lean management on the record.

Another tactic could be to elucidate the link between workplace stress endemic to classical management and employee health (Goh et al., 2016), and the great financial and non-financial costs that accrue to corporations, workers, and society. This causal story (Emiliani, 2015), more fact-based than distorted political narrative, could quickly enter public awareness and result in broad-based support for Lean management. Productive alliances could be established between corporations and groups (i.e. labor) that suffer from this problem and various organizations that have solutions to this problem (academics, healthcare providers, Lean organizations). This could greatly strengthen Lean management's footing and lead to effective populist political action (see Note 11).

If successful, the next step for classical management executives would be to learn the technical methods and behavioral routines necessary to succeed as a Lean leader (see Note 12). The traditional method of educating executives in Lean management will have to be thoroughly re-examined because it is well-known to produce little in the way of results. Simpler and more creative forms of executive training and education must be conceived and tested.

Workers, as well as professionals, will likely value the four future emotional representations as well (Table 2-3). Whether or not the future representation can actually or fully deliver on those promises to executives or workers is immaterial because, as a political problem, plausible alternative narratives are far more important than the facts. When consistently applied over many years, alternate narratives coupled with effective images become potent formulations for advancing political strategies.

An important part of the consistent messaging is to explain simply and convincingly why several methods contained in the CEO Wealth Creation Playbook are out of date and should be discontinued (see Note 13). Closing off these methods of wealth creation – particularly the ones most predatory and destructive to workers and society – will force executives to experiment with alternate methods, of which Lean management appears to be even better suited for future times than has been in the past. Executives are likely to find that alternative methods of wealth creation rooted in Lean management will yield more favorable outcomes for all interested parties.

A bedrock understanding in Lean management is that workers are valuable resources who, together with management, work together to improve the work – simplify the work, reduce burdens, make work more meaningful, and make it easier for workers to succeed (Byrne, 2012; Shook, 2015, 2017). In this way, Lean leaders elevate work and become more closely connected to it, rather than demean work and increase their distance from it as classical management does. The Lean view of valuing people and their work is an effective message and should be the basis for creating a grassroots political effort. This will pressure executives to reflect on the utility of politics, power, coercion, and predation, and perhaps give more serious consideration to Lean management. Politicians must be influenced as well because as a group, they too have demeaned work. They will have to confront the need to re-write laws permitting predatory business practices in favor of new laws that compel generative business practices, for which Lean management is well-suited. A populist movement may need to focus its initial efforts on politicians prior to influencing corporate leaders (see Note 14).

Summary

Like Scientific Management before it, the first 30 years of Lean management has experienced a mixed record, with far fewer examples of successful replacement of classical management with Lean management, and a far greater struggle for acceptance among executives of large corporations than was originally imagined. This is due to the decades-long view that acceptance for Lean management hinges on solutions to technocratic and behavioral problems. Instead, acceptance for Lean management is shown to be a political problem, reflective of the fundamental nature of business and corporations as political institutions first, followed by their function as economic institutions. As such, it requires a political solution.

Lean is at a cross-road. Thirty years have been invested in the economic institutional view of business and how Lean supports that view. The Lean movement can continue along that path and hope for better results in the future. Or, it can objectively analyze its failures, act upon that and other pertinent information, and craft a different path based on a new understanding of Lean as a political problem now that fundamental fault lines of conflicting interests in the practice management have been clearly exposed. Included within the fault lines are the parts of 18th and 19th century political economy that were carried forward to advance executive class interests and which diminished working class interests.

The effort mounted thus far to promote Lean has been pallid and insular, and must be elevated to a tough, boisterous, and respectful fight. It must confront the fact that when it comes to management practice, executive reasoning is not controlled by logic or intellect. Instead, it is controlled by habits, values, sentiments, and opinions held by the executive class, which clearly run along lines favorable to classical management: subordination, dependence, compliance, control, and exploit. Resistance to change is embedded in classical management and actively functions as a useful feature, rather than as a non-functioning vestigial feature, of predatory political control. As such, change cannot be brought into existence using only familiar concepts and methods.

Political solutions to polarizing political problems are not easy or inexpensive. And, admittedly, it is unclear if the timing is right for this type of political activism, whether a coalition can be established, or whether the level of funding or human engagement needed are attainable. Yet, one can clearly see how the past has imprinted itself on classical management practice and how political values and sentiments become heritable predispositions emulated across generations of executives.

One can also see how continuing in that same direction seems to be a poor choice. Poor choice or not, one should expect stiff resistance from entrenched interests as a well-organized challenge to classical management represents a normative threat. There is also the reality that a significant portion of the workforce may prefer classical management, as it relieves employees of certain workplace challenges and burdens.

If political solutions prove to be out of reach, or concurrently with political solutions, are there other ways that the great divide could be narrowed? Classical management executives see Lean management as an unwelcome disruption of the equilibrium condition that they carefully created. Lean management executives view change (improvement) as a welcome disruption that supports the evolutionary needs of business to assure adaptation and long-term survival. Each system of management is regarded as "the Truth" based upon executive's initial assumptions and subsequent confirming experiences, which leads to incessant and impersonal cross-talk, resulting in little or no progress toward narrowing the divide. Perhaps it is time to personalize the cross-talk by inviting executives who steadfastly support classical management to Lean management conferences, with executives from both schools presenting their views to better understand one another and to begin the process of de-stigmatizing progressive Lean management. Who knows what else might come of it (see Note 15 and 16)?

One wonders how prevalent Lean management might be today if it were understood from the start, thirty years ago, as a political problem rather than as an economic problem. Careful study of primary sources describing the decades-earlier rise and fall of Scientific Management might have made this apparent (see Note 17). This book is a call to action that will test the abilities and willpower of Lean community leaders to solve the problems identified.

Questions to Reflect On

- Is it possible that 20th century progressive management inadvertently strengthened classical management practice (and neoclassical economics)?
- How can the political values and sentiments of Lean management that offend adherents of classical management be ameliorated?
- How can Lean advocates and classical management adherents develop better understanding of one another (see Note 18)?
- How can Lean management be advanced without devastating the classical management practice to which so many executives understand and appreciate?
- In what ways could political action *for* Lean management create strong actions *against* Lean management?
- In what ways could business, the economy, and society be worse off if Lean was the dominant system of management?
- Causal stories about changes in the distributions of power and wealth have a poor record of success (see Note 19). What can be done to change that?
- How can small changes in the distribution of power and wealth be achieved without resorting to simplistic "good versus evil" or "us versus them" arguments?
- Is Lean management best left to those leaders who want it; where there is pull for Lean, and scale back efforts and investment in selling and marketing Lean?
- Progress always faces strong headwinds. Is widespread acceptance of Lean management a matter of time? Will it occur naturally, or does it need to be forced?

- What circumstance or event might occur in the future that could make classical management appear weak and ill-suited for continued use?

- If you were to describe classical management and Lean management in terms of musical genres, what would they be? Could such analogies be useful in gaining acceptance for Lean (see Note 20)?

Notes

1. Lean management is distinct from Toyota's management system (See Chapter 1, Figure 1-1). While the two share some similarities, they are different in numerous important ways (Monden, 1983; Ohno, 1988). Lean management and Toyota's management system are not synonymous. Whether Lean or TMS, it has proven to be enormously difficult to get executives to learn the principles and methods that all employees must practice. The difficulty apparently lies in the executive's view that having to learn new principles and methods is an unfair burden, one that conflicts with executive privilege, and is therefore illegitimate. It is more honorable to suffer a measure of hypocrisy than succumb to following instructions given by employees (or consultants) inferior in rank.

2. Both Professor Francis Wayland (b. 1796, d. 1865; fourth president of Brown University, Providence, Rhode Island, https://www.brown.edu/about/administration/president/people/past-presidents/francis-wayland-1827-1855) and Professor Aaron Chapin (b. 1817, d. 1892, first president of Beloit College, Beloit, Wisconsin, https://www.beloit.edu/archives/history/presidents/aaron_chapin/) were ministers who held Doctor of Divinity (D.D.) degrees. This reveals the intimate association between God and humankind in the pursuit of happiness and gratification resulting from one's self-directed labor, in harmony with their community. Classical political economy of the 19th century was inseparable from the organic life process given by God to humans; work and its resulting rewards are manifestations of God's will and benevolence.

3. In classical management, only the surface-level meaning of "Respect for People" is understood. Nevertheless, it is summarily rejected simply because it threatens corporate political hegemony. In Lean management, "Respect for People" has scores of deeper meanings which bring forward the full force of human capacity for learning and improving one's work day-by-day. In this way, "Respect for People" functions in part as an essential aid to long-term corporate survival. The opposite of "Respect for People," predation, also sustains corporate survival – though not necessarily for the long-term.

4. Micromanaging employees is a basic feature of classical management, in which those above visibly and audibly exert power (dominance) on those below. Lean management, as influenced by Toyota's management system, has a different view of power. The key to successful management is to lead as if one has no power, i.e. by stealth. Taiichi Ohno called this "management by ninjutsu" (Ohno, 1988, pp. 68-70). This approach to management obviously does not satisfy the political objectives of classical management. Another important difference between Lean management and classical management is how power is used. Once power is gained in classical management, its user is required to generate and exhibit successive exploits to accumulate and retain power, due to emulative and competitive pressures. Often, unnecessary exploits are invented to solidify and extend power, or merely to occupy one's time. The use of power to justify one's power is an irresponsible exercise of power. In Lean management, power must always be used responsibly. Lean is sober.

5. It is odd that preservation of corporate political interests far outweighs the need for organic improvement in business performance. For example, productivity (and hence, economic) growth is perpetually weak, on average, in organizations that practice classical management. Big, one-time gains are achieved by artificial means, such as layoffs, replacing workers with machines, outsourcing (or offshoring) work, and acquisitions. In Lean management, productivity gains are larger and consistent over time, and achieved by improving business processes via kaizen (Kato and Smalley, 2015; Emiliani et al., 2015; Wood et al., 2015) and related methods. Widespread adoption of Lean management is the best-known method for solving a company's (Byrne, 2012) and a nation's productivity problem, provided executives give labor its "just reward," year in and year out, as macroeconomic conditions permit. As Table 2-1 shows, this does not occur because mutual prosperity and fairness are foreign political values and sentiments in classical management. The trajectory of classical management is likely to remain constant, and therefore rapidly replace labor with new forms of machine technology such as robots and artificial intelligence because of executive's long-standing view that work is irksome, odious, unclean, menial, ignoble, and dirty. These new technologies are formidable competitors to Lean. Worth considering also is how artificial intelligence might incorporate (via software coding and subsequent machine learning) the political values and sentiments of classical management (Table 2-1), either purposefully or accidentally, as these values and sentiments are ingrained in the workers who write the software and build the machines, or training the machines via executive voice commands.

The power of the political values and sentiments of classical management to survive in different host environments should not be underestimated.

6. The political values and sentiments of Lean management shown in Table 2-1 can be quite problematic for those who are aligned with the political values and sentiments of classical management. They can appear to look suspiciously like liberal values and sentiments (e.g. social market economy), rather than classical or conservative values and sentiments (e.g. market capitalism). This immediately invokes skepticism or denial of Lean. It also casts suspicion on the people who created Lean and those who promote or advocate Lean, if not their outright dismissal. From the perspective of adherents to classical management, "improvement" sounds a lot like "reform," which sounds a lot like "revolution," which sounds a lot like "very bad" and "unacceptable." The conflict is between same and change, status quo and evolution, equilibrium and action, and conservation and transformation; a tangled knot of historical, political, economic, and social features, feelings, and facts against the innate human impulse to adapt, create, survive, and prosper. One can easily empathize with classical management executives who receive the Lean message as: 1) Your company's performance is bad and 2) You, the leaders, are the reason why corporate performance is bad. Benefits, such as improving the health of the company and its employees, do not resonate.

7. Acceptance was greatest among executives of mid-size enterprises who were open to learning from the Japanese sensei who helped develop Toyota's production system and

did not fear change (meaning, the amygdala's in their brain did not hijack their emotions and supersede logic and reason). This includes CEOs Arthur Byrne (Byrne, 2012), Dr. Gary Kaplan (Kenney, 2010), Pat Lancaster (Womack and Jones, 1996), George Koenigsaecker (president of Jacobs Manufacturing Company), George Sherman (CEO of Danaher), and some others, who fully embraced the teachings of kaizen consultants such as Chihiro Nakao (formerly, plant manager of Toyota parts supplier Taiho Kogyo Co., Ltd. and an assistant to Taiichi Ohno) of Shingijutsu USA (http://www.shingijutsuusa.com/) (Wood et al., 2015; Emiliani et al., 2015). Therefore, these CEOs were not specifically influenced by Lean as constructed and described by Womack and Jones (Womack and Jones, 1996), even though these executives may describe the changes that took place as a "Lean transformation."

8. To be precise, Lean is *mostly* rooted in facts, data, reality, and hence the advancement of logical and rational arguments. The promotion of Lean has seen its share of half-truths, misrepresentations, and hype. There has long been a tendency to highlight successes (usually limited in nature) and ignore failures – indicative of a plague of confirmation bias. See the blog posts "Lean Transformation Failure   Analysis"   (2   March   2016) https://bobemiliani.com/lean-transformation-failure-analysis/ and "Lean Success and Failure" (17 April 2016) https://bobemiliani.com/lean-success-and-lean-failure/.
With respect to political rhetoric, the leaders of the Lean community will have to decide whether it is better to be accurate (via rational empirical arguments) or better to win (via appeals to emotions and beliefs).

9. Sensei Toshihiro Nagamatsu of Shingijutsu USA says: "We are always at our worst. You may think you are a good company today, but make no mistake you are not. You may become better tomorrow, but still you are toward the back. At any moment, somewhere in this world there is someone doing the same work better. There is no end. You must continually seek to improve" (as recounted by Stacey Gleiss). This view of management responsibility, borne of Nagamatsu-san's experience working for Toyota, is both foreign and opposite the view of executives who embrace classical management values and sentiments (Table 2-1), and is thus rejected. If executives were to embrace Nagamatsu-san's wise words, the next barrier they would encounter is the complicated technical and behavioral routines of Lean management that they would have to learn in order to improve corporate performance – far more complicated than the CEO Wealth Creation Playbook. This provides yet another reason to reject Lean management. Political elites studiously avoid acknowledging their weaknesses so that they can evade the difficult work required of them to learn new thinking and practice new routines.

10. Where competition is defined as peer group companies residing at $\pm1.5\sigma$ in a normal distribution. The companies that reside at lower and higher standard deviations are usually ignored by executives.

11. Successful Lean management has therapeutic benefits to both managers and employees via the practice of simple yet effective daily routines that improve both the work and one's health. Lean management can be adopted by

executives as part of a wider strategy to improve the health and wellness of all employees and lower healthcare costs in organizations. To learn more, see "Lesson 66, People and Processes," "Lesson 67, Healthcare in Lean," and "Lesson 68, Don't be a Stress Raiser" in *Lean is Not Mean: 68 Practical lessons in Lean Leadership*, by Bob Emiliani, The CLBM, LLC, Wethersfield, Conn, 2015.

12. The technical methods and behavioral routines necessary to succeed as a Lean leader revolve around assuring that outcomes are non-zero-sum (win-win), versus the zero-sum (win-lose) outcomes that are foundational to the functioning of classical management. Part of the political solution lies in communicating to the grass roots that they should not accept zero-sum outcomes as minor offenses or inconveniences that are required for capitalism to function effectively. The teaching should include a pragmatic characterization of win-win to blunt unrealistic idealized versions of win-win. This could be simply stated as: "Win-win means you might not win as much as you would like, but you will not lose as much as you could." Balance is an important and omnipresent concept in Lean management, as is ensuring amends are made for those who have sacrificed to restore balance. By doing so, it assures the continued support and best efforts of stakeholders (business partners) to achieve shared outcomes such as mutual trust and mutual prosperity. In contrast, classical management seeks to create as great an imbalance as is politically possible, wherever it is possible.

13. The male-dominated executive ranks leads to a lack of diversity in how business problems are seen, resulting in a fixed set of solutions to any business problem (i.e. the CEO Wealth Creation Playbook) that minimizes the executive effort necessary to earn maximum rewards. This helps account for the durability and survivability of classical management and associated predatory instinct of political power, and highlights the pernicious nature of institutional prejudice against reform – despite the obvious need to evolve in step with changing times and let go of ancient or archaic preconceptions, values, and sentiments that prevent human and institutional adaptation.

14. In general, workers have real no power in a corporate setting compared to an electoral politics setting. They face near-certain dismissal if they strongly challenge management, both individually and particularly as an organized force – whether part of a labor union or not. Advocating for better processes and better management using the scientific methods unfortunately carries enormous risk in corporate environments governed by political methods. However, a citizen's ability to vote confers great power that can lead to substantial changes in representation and related interests. One might suppose that an alternate, and perhaps better, route for change would be through corporate boards of directors. Boards could require CEOs to adopt Lean, or employees (as shareholders through 401(k) plans or other stockholding arrangements) could vote for an alternate slate of candidate directors. The former is unlikely to happen because board members are Cerberus-like guardians of vested rights and interests (guardians of "the dead hand of the Vested Interests," as Veblen put it).

For the latter case, the corporate constitution or bylaws could be quickly re-written to change how board members are chosen. The author knows of no circumstance where a board of directors dismissed a CEO or president because of their failure to adopt Lean management as directed. The author is aware of the reverse (many cases, via AB), wherein the CEO or president refused to heed the board's directive to adopt Lean management in its full form and suffered no consequence. Boards often fail to take decisive action against delinquent CEOs or presidents – often for years – because they fear numerous and varied consequences. Given these constraints, people often turn to the educational system as the solution, beginning in grade school and through to graduate school. As far as concerns higher education, there is an extraordinarily strong bias against hiring academically qualified faculty who have significant business experience. And, as is commonly known, you must have practiced Lean management to be competent in teaching it in business school or engineering school; much like one must practice surgery to teach surgery in medical school. Such is the great power of the "Guardians of Vested Interests" (Veblen, 1921).

15. In classical management practice, a company's existence is a fleeting concept, with not much thought given to demise by its own or other hands ("creative destruction," poor decisions, or neglect, as the case may be). In general, classical management rewards management idleness (slow rate of change or evolution) and punishes those who see big problems and advocate for action or who take swift action. A company's failure causes great upheaval to employees and their families, suppliers, customers, investors, and

communities. Invariably, executives describe the mass layoffs and plant closings as "painful but necessary." I describe mass layoffs and plant closings as "predictable and avoidable." The view among Lean management executives is that such calamities must be avoided, and that the company's existence is not ephemeral or guided by the hand of fate. Management idleness is not rewarded, and people are rewarded for seeing problems and taking action (rapid rate of change or evolution). This difference in understanding could be one of several useful perspectives that classical management executives might welcome. Lean management offers many other practical business teachings that are common to the interests of classical management executives. Corporate failure analysis and how to improve the probability of long-term survival could be a helpful bridge between the two management ideologies. See the blog post "Prof. Emiliani's A4 Failure Analysis Method" (4 March 2016), https://bobemiliani.com/prof-emilianis-a4-failure-analysis-method/.

16. Taiichi Ohno and his team successfully convinced people that a manufacturing worker's movement is not entirely comprised of work. He expressed it this way (Ohno, 1988, p. 58): Let's assume the work an operator performs is movement. Upon careful observation, one finds that moving does not mean an operator is working (Figure A-1); i.e. "actually advancing the process towards completing the job." A substantial portion of what an operator does is comprised of waste (doing anything unnecessary) and non-value-added work that is necessary (NVA-N) *under current conditions*, and only a small amount of net work (Figure A-2).

Typically, the sum of Type I and Type II waste is about 90 percent.

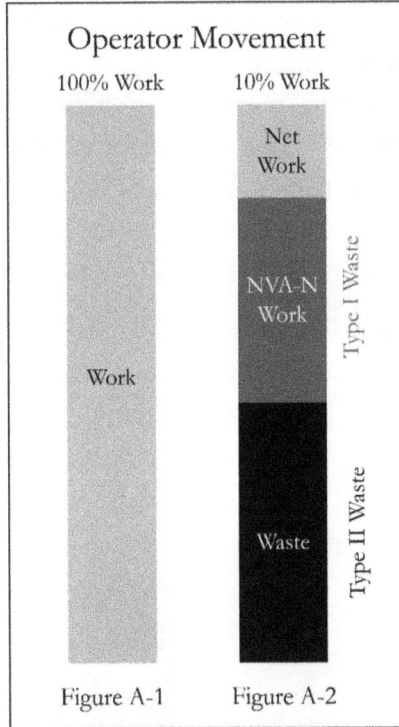

Figure A-1   Figure A-2

The primary objective of process improvement is to first eliminate waste (Type II), as well as unevenness and unreasonableness, (usually) followed by eliminating non-value-added but necessary work (Type I waste). As a result, almost the entirety of operator movement is work, thus creating the "full-work" system (for transforming material). By doing so, operator productivity can be increased 200 to 500 percent or more, while simplifying the operator's work and making it less burdensome.

We have an analogous situation when it comes to what executives do. Let's assume the work an executive performs is thinking. Upon careful observation, one finds that thinking does not mean an executive is working (Figure B-1); i.e., "actually advancing the process* towards completing the job." A substantial portion of what an executive does is comprised of waste (doing anything unnecessary) and non-value-added work that is necessary (NVA-N) *under current conditions*, and only a small amount of net work (Figure B-2). The sum of Type I and Type II waste is also about 90 percent.

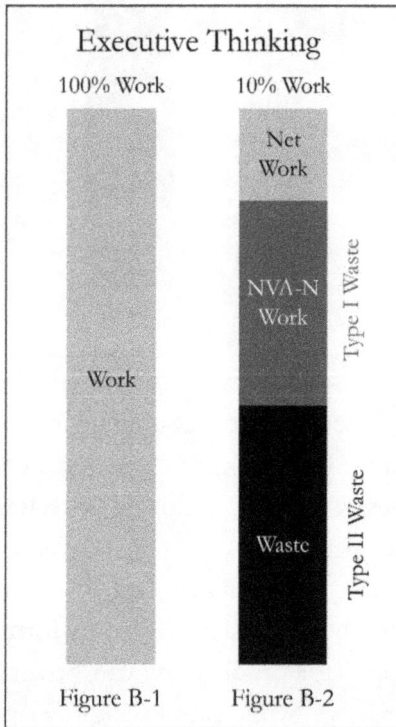

Executive Thinking

100% Work   10% Work

Net Work

NVA-N Work   Type I Waste

Work

Waste   Type II Waste

Figure B-1   Figure B-2

As Chapters 1 and 2 have shown, executive thinking is dominated by Type I and Type II waste (informed by both tangible and spiritual relics of the long-ago past), resulting in little net work. Isn't it sensible to improve executive thinking so that productivity can be similarly increased, while also simplifying the executive's work and making it less burdensome? A "full-work" system for executives (transforming information) could be another area of common interest.

---

* To understand executive work as process work, see *Speed Leadership: A New Way to Lead for Rapidly Changing Times*, by B. Emiliani, The CLBM, LLC, Wethersfield, Conn., 2015

17. While the history of Scientific Management is extremely useful to help understand what has transpired with Lean management over the last 30 years, the are some notable differences. In particular, the types of major defects. In Scientific Management, the major defect was its prescriptive nature. Meaning, the requirement to impose strict rules and strict methods for the "installation" and operation of Scientific Management in a company. Most company executives would not accept that. Lean has gone in the other direction. It major defect could turn out to be its descriptive nature. Meaning, the view that each organization is unique, and that their problems and solutions are therefore unique (referred to as "situational problems"). Most company executives can accept that, but what it results in is innumerable different and heavily diluted forms of Lean that have little or no actual business impact. It has been said that copying is the most common failure mode of Lean transformation, and therefore one should not copy

what other people or organizations have done (see https://www.lean.org/LeanPost/Posting.cfm?LeanPostId= 829, minute 12:30 to 13:30). There are three problems with this view: First, there is a difference between good copying and bad copying. At the macro-level, it is clear that bad copying is the most common failure mode of Lean transformation – what I long-ago termed "fake Lean." On the other hand, good copying has resulted in some of the most noteworthy Lean transformations. Jacobs, Lantech, Wiremold, Autoliv, Virginia Mason, etc., coincidentally all were facilitated by former Toyota engineers or managers. Second, to not copy others presupposes a level of sophistication (knowledge and experience) that most managers do not possess. In other words, they do not know enough to not copy. Is that bad? No; copying helps orient people in the right direction at the start. For example, artists begin their studies by copying the work, style, and technique of others, and continue doing that until such time they have developed sufficient understanding and skill to create their own style and technique. Third, the long training that an artist undergoes represents a long sustained and high level of commitment that is rarely found in within a company's management when it comes to Lean. Most often, the highest level of commitment is found in the cadre of top-tier consultants who were trained by former Toyota managers. So, most companies have no choice but to copy from the start – and the fundamental business problems are almost always the same three things: cost, quality, and delivery (or lead-time). The question is whether management committed to make a good copy or a bad copy? Returning to the original thought: Scientific Management was prescriptive while Lean management has been descriptive. In the most successful Lean transformations, it has been a balance of both prescriptive and descriptive. The defects are ameliorated through compromise. There is much to be learned from that.

18. This will be a bigger challenge than is apparent from reading Chapters 1 and 2, because the habitual basis for reasoning and the habitual method of reasoning in classical management and Lean management are completely different. The former is abstract and political (i.e. metaphysical and by right) and Lean management is real and scientific (i.e. factual and objective). Said in another, simpler, way, the engineer (and scientist) is subservient to the business leader. What is the basis for disturbing that customary and universal order?

19. The reaction to changes in the distribution of power and wealth – even small changes – arouses deep passions and generates great tumult. Those with vested rights and interests decry potential losses and comprehensively resist change, while those who might benefit are considered parasitic and free riders (wanting something for nothing). In fact, vested rights and interests essentially define the doctrine of wanting something for nothing, which is seen only as good and right when the situation is reversed. These ideological battles are as old as the time when vainglorious leaders separated themselves from their social groups and claimed ownership rights to tribal resources. Deep passions are evident in other ways. One can, as I have long done, write trade books and academic papers using the words "executive" and "worker" and receive no judgment. But, writing the words "executive **class**" and "worker **class**"

invites swift judgment – and which is routinely off-target. Passion is as much an instrument to maintain equilibrium (vested rights and interests) as it is an instrument of change. 20. Like many others, my experience with progressive management has been more fun and energizing than classical management, which is staid, stifling, and lacks the human touch. When it is successful, the music genre I associate with Lean management is electronic dance music (EDM). It is creative, rhythmic, energetic, and fun, and it gets people off their asses and onto the dance floor (the genba!) where they do something useful. And, it is inspiring because you don't have to be a musician to create EDM – just like you don't have to be an industrial engineer to improve processes. The music genre I associate with classical management is – what else – classical music; specifically, romantic music (1820-1915) and its characteristic traits (see https://en.wikipedia.org/wiki/Romantic_music). It also happens to be the era in which political economy and the practice of classical management in corporations became formalized. A coincidence?

References

Ballé, M., Jones, D., Chaize, J., and Fiume, O. (2017), *The Lean Strategy: Using Lean to Create Competitive Advantage, Unleash Innovation, and Deliver Sustainable Growth*, McGraw Hill Education, New York, NY

Barry, M. (2017), "Leadership in an Age of Disruption," 7 September, In Business – Madison, http://www.ibmadison.com/Blogger/Open-Mic/September-2017/Leadership-in-an-age-of-disruption/, accessed 25 December 2017

Bower, J. and Paine, L. (2017) "The Error at the Heart of Corporate Leadership," *Harvard Business Review*, Vol. 95, No. 3, May-June Issue, pp. 50-60, https://hbr.org/2017/05/managing-for-the-long-term#the-error-at-the-heart-of-corporate-leadership, accessed 21 December 2017

Byrne, A. (2012), *The Lean Turnaround: How Business Leaders Use Lean Principles to Create Value and Transform Their Company*, McGraw Hill Education, New York, NY

Emiliani, B. (2011), *Moving Forward Faster: The Mental Evolution from Fake Lean to REAL Lean*, The CLBM, LLC, Wethersfield, Conn.

Emiliani, B. (2015), *Lean is Not Mean: 68 Practical lessons in Lean Leadership*, The CLBM, LLC, Wethersfield, Conn., pp. 265-299

Emiliani, B., Yoshino, K., and Go, R. (2015), *Kaizen Forever: Teachings of Chihiro Nakao*, The CLBM, LLC, Wethersfield, Conn.

Goh, J., Pfeffer, J., and Stefanos, Z., (2016), "The Relationship Between Workplace Stressors and Mortality and Health Costs in the United States," *Management Science*, Vol. 62, Issue 2, pp. 608-628

"Goodman, P. (2017), "The Robots are Coming, and Sweden is Fine," *The New York Times*, 27 December, https://www.nytimes.com/2017/12/27/business/the-robots-are-coming-and-sweden-is-fine.html, accessed 27 December 2017

Kato, I. and Smalley, A. (2011), *Toyota Kaizen Methods: Six Steps to Improvement*, CRC Press, Boca Raton, Florida

Kenney, C. (2010), *Transforming Health Care: Virginia Mason Medical Center's Pursuit of the Perfect Patient Experience*, CRC Press, Boca Raton, Florida

Krafcik, J.F. (1988), "Triumph of the Lean Production System," *Sloan Management Review*, Vol. 30, No. 1, pp. 41-52

McGregor, D. (1960), *The Human Side of Enterprise*, McGraw-Hill, New York, NY

Monden, Y. (1983), *Toyota Production System: Practical Approach to Production Management*, Engineering and Management Press, Norcross, Georgia

Ohno, T. (1988), *Toyota Production System – Beyond Large-Scale Production*, Productivity Press, Portland, Oregon

Person, H. (Ed.) in Taylor, F.W. (1947), *Scientific Management: Comprising Shop Management, Principles of Scientific Management, Testimony Before the House Committee*, H. Person, Ed., Harper & Brothers Publishers, New York, NY, p. xii

Plotkin, S. and Tilman, R. (2011), *The Political ideas of Thorstein Veblen*, Yale University Press, New Haven, Conn.

Shook, J. (2015), "Work," John Shook's eLetters, Lean Enterprise Institute, 11 June, https://www.lean.org/shook/DisplayObject.cfm?o=2999, accessed 23 December 2017

Shook, J. (2017), "Want Better Employees? Be a Better Employer.," John Shook's eLetters, Lean Enterprise Institute, 7 December, https://www.lean.org/shook/DisplayObject.cfm?o=2999, accessed 23 December 2017

Stone, D. (1989), "Causal Stories and the Formation of Policy Agendas," *Political Science Quarterly*, Vol. 104, No. 2, pp. 281-300

Taylor, F. W. (1911), *The Principles of Scientific Management*, Harper and Brothers, New York, NY

Teggart, R.V. (1932), *Thorstein Veblen: A Chapter in American Economic Thought*, University of California Press, Berkeley, California

Veblen, T. (1899), *The Theory of the Leisure Class: An Economic Study of Institutions*, Macmillan Co., New York, NY

Veblen, T. (1904), *The Theory of Business Enterprise*, Charles Scribner's Sons, New York, NY

Veblen, T. (1914), *The Instinct of Workmanship: And the State of the Industrial Arts*, The Macmillan Company, New York, NY

Veblen, T. (1921), *The Engineers and the Price System*, B.W. Huebsch, Inc., New York, NY

Wayland, F. (1885), *The Elements of Political Economy*, recast by A. L. Chapin, Sheldon and Company, New York, NY (First edition published in 1837)

Womack, J., Jones, D., and Roos, D. (1990), *The Machine that Changed the World*, Rawson Associates, New York, NY

Womack, J. and Jones, D. (1996), *Lean Thinking: Banish Waste and Create Wealth in Your Corporation: The Story of Lean Production*, Simon & Schuster, New York, NY

Womack, J.P. (2017), "Jim Womack on Where Lean Has Failed and Why Not to Give Up," *Planet Lean: The Lean Global Network Journal*, 29 August, http://planet-lean.com/jim-womack-on-where-lean-has-failed-and-why-not-to-give-up, accessed 21 December 2017

Womack, J.P. (2017a), "Create Stable, Fulfilling Jobs to Fully Benefit from Lean," *Planet Lean: The Lean Global Network Journal*, 30 October, http://planet-lean.com/create-stable-fulfilling-jobs-to-fully-benefit-from-lean, accessed 22 December 2017

Wood, R., Herscher, M., and Emiliani, B. (2015), *Shingijutsu-Kaizen: The Art of Discovery and Learning*, The CLBM, LLC, Wethersfield, Conn.

Woollard, F. G., and Emiliani, B. (2009), *Principles of Mass and Flow Production*, 55th Anniversary Special Reprint Edition, The CLBM, LLC, Wethersfield, Conn. (Original date of publication of *Principles of Mass and Flow Production*:1954)

3
Metaphysical CEOs
and
Lean Management

Abstract

Chapter 1 identified executive culture as the animating source of resistance to Lean management in large corporations. Chapter 2 showed that acceptance for Lean management was a political problem, not the technocratic or behavioral problem it has long been thought to be. Chapter 3 seeks to connect these two findings to a third causal condition allied with classical management practice: metaphysical leadership. This chapter examines the generic metaphysical disposition and propensities of CEOs and its effects within companies and on external stakeholders. A mechanism is proposed by which corporate leaders abandon their understanding of the material realm of work and begin to apprehend a distant metaphysical understanding of workers and work processes. Concomitant with this change is a transformation of executive reasoning from *de facto* to *de jure*. The combination of the three causal conditions result in stasis, where equilibrium is sought after and more highly prized than evolution into modern Lean management practice. A preferred method for disrupting the equilibrium of classical management to aid the advancement of Lean management is identified.

Note: This chapter explores the research question: Why are executives disinterested in Lean management?

Introduction

A fundamental problem in the change-over from one long-established system of management, classical management, to newer system of progressive management, Lean management, is gaining the acceptance and participation of the top executive and their direct reports. Despite the logical and rational presentations of Lean management and its associated benefits, the vast majority of executives have, over the last 30 years, declined to adopt Lean management in its full form. Instead, many choose to adopt highly diluted forms limited to a handful of Lean methods or tools that they perceive will assist workers and make a small contribution to improving business performance.

This difficulty has long been known to the creators and promoters of progressive management systems (Person, 1947; Ohno, 1988; Womack, 2017). Yet, the specific sources of executive resistance and the specific factors that prevent acceptance unknown until they were identified in Chapters 1 and 2. They illuminate the complex and interdependent features of executive culture that form a bulwark against the intrusion of Lean management and the recognition that acceptance of Lean is neither a technocratic nor a behavioral problem, but a political problem. However, there is a missing piece. Namely, the mechanism that animates and perpetuates this phenomenon.

Employees who are close to the actual work of processing material and information are generally less resistant and quicker to accept progressive Lean management than are executives. However, executives were, early in their career, close to the actual work processes, and should be able to see its benefits. What changed? More importantly, how did the change occur? What is the specific mechanism that generates the change? No such mechanism has been previously identified. This chapter seeks to correct that by offering a plausible mechanism by which executives transition from understanding the material realm of work – facts, processes, and cause-and-effect – to apprehending a distant, metaphysical, or spiritual (theoretical or abstract) understanding of the work.

The problem statement that this chapter pursues is as follows:

> What is the mechanism by which business leaders abandon their understanding of the material realm of work to apprehend a distant metaphysical understanding of the work?

Related to this is the role of the scientific method and critical thinking embedded in the material realm of work processes. Today, it is common for the top executive to have obtained undergraduate and graduate degrees in technical, social science, or liberal arts fields that require them to learn, over many years of practice, the scientific method or critical thinking. This is in addition to the critical thinking habits and methods that they learned and practiced from grade school through high school. Graduates enter the workforce and nominally apply these methods to their work. But, they abandon these habits and methods as they rise through the management hierarchy. Why?

This chapter explores the generic transition from a worker who thinks and reasons critically and is fact-based, grounded in the material realm of processes and cause-and-effect, to a business leader who thinks and reasons in pecuniary and political terms. This is shown to constitute a transition to the metaphysical realm. Specifically, the phenomenon whereby *de facto* reasoning (reasoning based processes that exist in reality; cause-and-effect) is replaced with *de jure* reasoning (reasoning based on rules, policies, or laws that largely do not exist in reality; spiritual). This generates an alternative problem statement:

What is the mechanism by which a future leader transforms their reasoning from *de facto* to *de jure*?

The following example illustrates the problem: A person earns bachelor, master, and doctoral degrees in science or engineering and then takes a job doing work in their field of study. They work in a company whose leaders practice classical management. They dutifully apply the scientific method to their work for a decade or so. Then, they get promoted and become a supervisor, followed by promotions to mid-level manager and then to executive. As they progress the management hierarchy, they quickly lose their habits and skills in the application of the scientific method (*de facto* reasoning) and adopt the pecuniary and political thought processes of their peers (*de jure* reasoning). They soon become habituated in *de jure* reasoning and are unable to comprehend or unwilling to acknowledge *de facto* reasoning – e.g. that given to them by employees in presentations. In the context of this chapter, it would be the logical and rational arguments put forward by people who promote Lean management internal or external to the company. As a result, the dedicated, time-consuming, and expensive efforts to advance Lean management largely fails (see Note 1).

This chapter assumes that Lean management must be led the top executive – the CEO or president (hereafter, CEO), and their direct reports, because it is a top-down and comprehensive change-over from classical management practice to Lean management practice (Emiliani et al, 2007, pp. 248-255), not a bottom-up change. A large body of empirical evince supports this assumption. However. This assumption does not preclude the possibility of grass-roots, bottom-up change, though this is unlikely given executives' predilection for the exercise of power and control, as well as interests that differ markedly from those of workers.

The Executive as Layman

Long ago, the owners of businesses were close to the worker and the work processes that generated revenue and profits. Owners typically acted as operators, performing the work processes themselves and carefully overseeing processes performed by employees, aided by their intimate first-hand knowledge of the process. Their close proximity to the work required owners to think first in terms of *de facto* reasoning – facts, processes, and cause-and-effect – and secondarily in terms of money.

In his book *The Instinct of Workmanship* (Veblen, 1914), Thorstein Veblen attributed the separation of managers from the workers and their work to two factors that emerged during the mid-to-late 1800s: 1) the increasing complexity of machine and process technologies, and 2) owners' increasing focus on money, which resulted in greater specialization of the managerial function. As a result, managers lost sight of the industrial work and technical processes that made the money. Veblen was harshly critical of this separation and viewed it as clear evidence of mismanagement of the enterprise. Veblen noted that the "efficiency engineers" hired by the top executive were close to the work and could easily see all the problems, yet the businessman's pecuniary focus resulted in a "trained inability" to comprehend the efficiency engineers' findings and advice for improving operations (p. 193):

> "If the 'efficiency engineers' are to be credited, it is probably within the mark to say that the net aggregate gains from industry fall short of what they might be by some fifty per cent, owing to the trained inability of the businessmen in control to appreciate and give effect to the visible technological requirements of the industries from which they draw their gain. To appreciate the kind and degree of this commonplace mismanagement of industry it is only necessary to contrast the facility, circumspection, shrewd strategy and close economy shown by these same businessmen in the organization and management of their pecuniary, fiscal and monetary operations, as against the waste of time, labour and materials that abounds in the industries under their control."

Veblen continues (p. 222):

> "It is the testimony of these efficiency engineers
> that relatively few pecuniary captains in command
> of industrial enterprises have a sufficient
> comprehension of the technological facts to
> understand and accept the findings of the
> technological experts who so argue for the
> elimination of preventable wastes, even when the
> issue is presented statistically in terms of price."

Thus, the rational and logical arguments used by the
"efficiency engineers" proved unconvincing to
businessmen, due largely to the separation between
management and the industrial processes. Veblen contrasts
this with how the top company managers in the earlier days
of industry were closer to the technologies of industrial
work processes (p. 224):

> "That the business community is so permeated with
> incapacity and lack of insight in technological
> matters is doubtless due proximately to the fact that
> their attention is habitually directed to the pecuniary
> issue of industrial enterprise; but more
> fundamentally and unavoidably it is due to the large
> volume and intricate complications of the current
> technological scheme, which will not permit any
> man to become a competent specialist in an alien
> and exacting field of endeavour, such as business
> enterprise, and still acquire and maintain an
> effectual and working acquaintance with the state of
> the industrial arts."

The result is business that is run by laypersons; leaders who do not possess the professional or specialized knowledge of technical work processes. So detrimental was this to the functioning of business that its efficiency was orders of magnitude lower than it should be. According to Veblen (Veblen, 1921, p. 68):

> "So that wherever the production experts are now taking over the management, out of the dead hand of the self-made captains, and wherever they have occasions to inquire into the established conditions of production, they find the ground cumbered with all sorts of incredible makeshifts of waste and inefficiency – such makeshifts as would perhaps pass muster with any moderately stupid elderly layman, but which look like blindfold guesswork to these men who know something of advanced technology and its working-out."

Veblen continues (pp. 70-71):

> "And all the while it is an open secret that with a reasonably free hand the production experts would today readily increase the ordinary output of industry by several fold, – variously estimated at some 300 per cent. to 1200 per cent. of the current output. And what stands in the way of so increasing the ordinary output of goods and services is business as usual."

Where "business as usual" means the continued separation of management from industrial process and money as the sole measure of efficiency for every process and every transaction. It means no change; a static or equilibrium condition is management's preferred state of business. Veblen continues (pp. 72-73):

> "During the opening yeas of the new [20th] century a lively interest centered on the views and expositions of these two groups of industrial experts [Scientific management experts and consulting engineers]; and not least was the interest aroused by their exhibits of current facts indicating an all-pervading lag, leak, and friction in the industrial system, due to its disjointed and one-eyed management..."

Indifference to industrial processes and process improvement reduced executives to layman status. All they knew was the highly specialized skill of running a business according to a small set of economic preconceptions, and did that so poorly as to underperform in terms of satisfying the needs of society and risking the survival of the business. Instead of improving efficiency, the limited and diminishing capabilities of the layman executive over time resulted in expansion of the "lag, leak, and friction" in all industrial processes. Thus, the transition to *de jure* reasoning begins by separating managers from the worker and their work processes.

It is worth contemplating for a moment one's personal experience as a worker and the separation between executives and the work processes in classical management. For example, it is commonplace for shop floor and office workers to never see the top executive or their direct reports in their work area. They are ensconced in private quarters and protected by their staff and loyal administrative aides. It is common to give presentations to executives based on facts, only to be challenged or rebuffed by various illogical, elliptical, tangential, or incomprehensible statements. It is also common to have to shape one's fact-based narrative to fit the boss's social, economic, or political affections and biases to gain consideration or acceptance (i.e. "you have to make them think they thought of it"). How common it is to explain to executives the work processes performed in current state value stream maps and hear them say: "I had no idea."

Workers are maddened by the complex machinations they must go through to communicate simple *de facto* (material) reasoned information to convoluted and esoteric *de jure* (metaphysical) reasoning recipients. It not only takes much longer time than is necessary, but it also diminishes the quality and accuracy of the information being conveyed, which, in turn, results in poor as well as delayed executive decision-making.

Importantly, separating executives from the workers and their work processes results in stasis; they see no need for processes to evolve and improve, nor do they see the need for training and developing workers' skills and capabilities. These are among the serious ramifications of businesses led by lay persons trained in classical management, where equilibrium is more prized than evolution.

Entering the Metaphysical Realm

The layman executive is a simple way of characterizing a more complex phenomenon: the metaphysical leader that is nearly ubiquitous in classical management. What is meant by "metaphysical" and what is a metaphysical leader? "Meta" means "after." So "metaphysical" means "after the physical," and "physical" means the material realm of work – its facts, processes, and cause-and-effect.

When promoted to supervisor, and especially beyond to manager and executive, the employee leaves the material realm due to their separation from workers and the work processes, which become transformed into a distant, metaphysical – philosophical, spiritual, abstract, or theoretical – understandings beyond the physical (material) realm and beyond human sense perception such that they are not verifiable by science (i.e. experimentally testable). They have become metaphysical leaders.

Compliance to the shared beliefs, language, and *de jure* reasoning create powerful in-group social bonds which result in management practice that is static and resistant to change. Lacking an evolutionary drive due to the absence of the scientific method and critical thinking, combined with shared beliefs, language, and *de jure* reasoning, inform executive actions which are typically detrimental to the workers and the work processes, and often to customers as well. Full attention given to the pecuniary philosophy of business assures the root of all problems are ignored, leading to a repetition of problems whose solution is mere re-cycling of the same shared beliefs, language, and *de jure* reasoning.

The industriousness of workers' tasks requires them to think in non-money terms: process, facts, observation, and cause-and-effect. Their continued employment depends on their ability to execute the task with few or no errors. Classical management calls leaders, exempt from work in the material realm, towards thinking in pecuniary terms, as well as in spiritual terms of reputation and inanimate objects such as budgets and headcount. This major transformation is initiated by a change in responsibilities from making or producing things (consuming resources) to leading (guarding resources). As might be expected, metaphysical leaders' continued employment is independent of the ability to execute tasks with few or no errors (Emiliani, 2015).

Exemption from work in the material realm launches managers into the metaphysical realm, in which leadership development is conditioned and habituated by their social environment, their daily activities, their responsibilities, and the discrete results that they are expected to achieve. The focus of leader's metaphysical realm is objects and compartmentalized outcomes, not the holistic and integrated processes that they are engaged in (Koskela and Kagioglou, 2006; Emiliani, 2015). The metaphysical leader's realm is summarized in Table 3-1:

The metaphysical elements assigned to leaders belong to them, but they are not actually theirs; they must make-believe they belong to them and do with them the best that

Table 3-1: Metaphysical Leader's Realm

Metaphysical Element	Activity or Concern
Budget	Money
Performance	Metrics
Labor	Meetings, E-mail
Location	Office, Conference Rooms
Information Source	Boss, Hierarchy
Communication	Recitation of Business Language
Policies and Rules	Company/Owners' Interests
Domain of Supervision	Headcount, Space, System, Equipment
Allegiance	Company, Boss
Personal Worth (status)	Loyalty, Income

they can. The daily execution of the metaphysical elements soon become a habit of mind and solidify inviolable rules for future actions. This completes the conversion to *de jure* (abstract) reasoning, which beneficially informs the political (versus scientific) method of decision-making. This, in turn, leads to exploit of all stakeholders at various times, whether it is intended or not – a characteristic habit of mind in classical management.

As an unskeptical, unquestioning functionary representing owners' vested rights and interests, the typical metaphysical leader's stated cause of "customer satisfaction" conceals two layers of purpose: to satisfy one's personal interests within the guise of satisfying owners' interests. The metaphysical realm, after all, is a domain of the obscure and ambiguous. The lack of clarity assures the development of specialized executive skills that are useful only in classical management. Imagine a CEO who has 25 or more years of daily experience in the metaphysical realm. Their habituation makes it nearly impossible to replace archaic management practice with newer forms of progressive management practice. One ensconced in the metaphysical realm, is it difficult to get out.

Workers do not know they enter the metaphysical realm when they are promoted to supervisor and beyond (Figure 3-1). They are unaware that it is happening, nor do they understand what it means or its consequences to one's self, other people, the business, or society. Simply by becoming disconnected from workers and work processes, and usually through no ill intention, supervisors and managers become unwitting impediments to progress. It is at the higher levels of leadership where being an impediment to progress is seen as both virtuous and valorous.

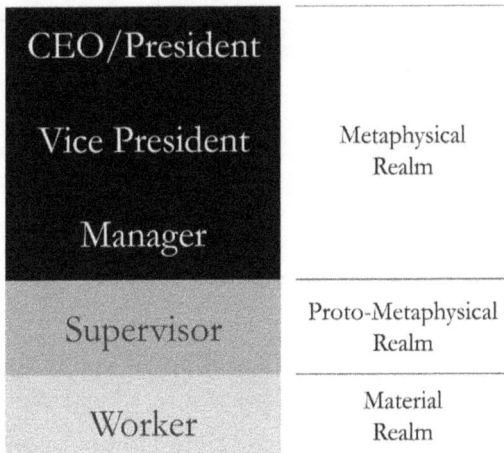

CEO/President	
Vice President	Metaphysical Realm
Manager	
Supervisor	Proto-Metaphysical Realm
Worker	Material Realm

Figure 3-1. Entrance into the metaphysical realm through successive advancement in organizations.

Recall the problem statements:

> What is the mechanism by which business leaders abandon their understanding of the material realm of work to apprehend a distant metaphysical understanding of the work?

> What is the mechanism by which a future leader transforms their reasoning from *de facto* to *de jure*?

The mechanism by which an employee becomes a metaphysical leader suffused with *de jure* reasoning is by:

1. Identify candidate leaders
2. Promote candidate leaders
3. Separate leaders from workers and the work
4. Assign metaphysical elements to leaders
5. Monitor compliance to metaphysical elements
6. Advance compliant leaders

This process makes it nearly impossible for leaders to understand, learn, and practice Lean management.

Metaphysical Leaders

The term "leadership" is recognized as the singular, top-level taxonomic category under which various styles of leadership are classified. The commonly recognized styles of leadership include (Eagly and Johannesen-Schmidt, 2001):

- Autocratic
- Bureaucratic
- Charismatic
- Democratic
- Laissez-faire
- Participative
- Paternalistic
- Transactional
- Transformational

This characterization is incomplete. The term "leadership" can be divided into two top-level taxonomic categories: one for the styles of leadership that conform to metaphysical leadership and another for the styles of leadership that conform to material leadership. The two leadership archetypes are shown in Table 3-2:

Table 3-2 Division of Leadership Styles

Leadership: Metaphysical	Leadership: Material
Autocratic	Democratic
Bureaucratic	(participative)
Charismatic	Servant
Laissez-faire	Transformational
Paternalistic	
Transactional	

Metaphysical leadership styles are rooted in a static, archaic philosophy of business (money-making) based on 18th and 19th century moral philosophy and political economy (e.g. Adam Smith, John Stuart Mill, David Ricardo). They adhere to the preconceptions of natural philosophy (i.e. natural liberty, natural rights, natural law), self-interest, laissez-faire, and unbridled profit-seeking to name a few. These philosophical tenets of business are rationalized into continued existence and their perpetuation requires an indifference to the material realm (facts, observation, process, cause-and-effect). The executive's uncritical eye thus disables needed progress (see Note 2). The rejection of progress and the acceptance of equilibrium induced by archaic *de jure* thinking strengthens over time until, as CEO, facts emanating from the material realm are no longer relevant or persuasive, thus signaling the complete development of the metaphysical leader.

Archaic elements of 18th and 19th century moral philosophy and political economy do not result in freedom. Instead they result in intellectual imprisonment and collective stasis, disabling all education in critical thinking and fact-based reality.

Conversely, material leadership styles demand attention to the material realm, which includes the humans that function with it, as individuals perform the work processes. Material leadership abandons or modifies the archaic philosophy of business (preconceptions) to better align corporate economic interests with the interests of each stakeholder and society at large.

It is unsurprising that there are more styles of metaphysical leadership than there are material leadership styles, and that they are more popular. Executives are the human representatives of metaphysical phenomena whose purpose is to limit the internal rate of change and handicap an organization's ability to adapt and improve work processes as conditions change. Importantly, metaphysical leadership suffers from poor and blocked information flows, resulting in pervasive inaccurate or false information that then leads to poor executive decision-making.

For such conditions to exist over long periods of time, metaphysical leaders must be guided by spiritual beliefs which inform *de jure* reasoning. These spiritual beliefs include:

- Invisible hand
- Laissez-faire
- Self-interest
- Growth
- Budgets
- Forecasts
- Money
- Economies of scale
- Vision
- Passion
- Intuition ("sixth sense")
- Certitude
- Opinions taken as facts
- Comparison as a basis for action (copying other leaders)
- Infallibility (in decision-making)
- Leisure ("time is on our side")
- Success (preordained through confirmation bias)
- Failure (unimaginable; impossible)

- Loyalty (among direct reports)
- Information accuracy
- Information security (secrets)
- Gossip and innuendo

These spiritual beliefs join together to create confusion between reality and appearance, which easily lead to misrepresentations or outright fabrications of the actual condition of the business and business results (Gryta, 2018). Lies, typically impossible to prove, are attributed to bad judgment, and described as the same kind of judgment that any other leader would make under similar circumstances. When decisions do not work out as planned, causal theories are quickly generated to explain away the problems. These causal theories, presented as fact, are attributed to the following generic causes (Stone, 1989):

Intentional Causes
- Rogue employee
- "A few bad apples"
- Policy or procedure not followed

Accidental
- Weather
- Natural disaster
- Machine failure

Inadvertent
- Unforeseen event
- Neglect
- Carelessness

- Omission

The construction of unverifiable or obfuscatory, yet believable-sounding, causal stories is consistent with the spiritual beliefs which inform the faulty *de jure* reasoning characteristic of classical management.

The effect is executive control of appearance, rather than executive comprehension of fact. Business philosophy (money-making) controls human industriousness (work); *de jure* reasoning controls *de facto* reasoning. In Lean businesses (exemplified by Toyota's management system; see Note 3), the opposite is true.; human industriousness, *de facto* reasoning, controls the business (*de jure* reasoning). This is not a small difference, nor is it a difference that one should ignore.

De facto reasoning among workers and managers results in better processes which lead to better and more consistent business results such as:

- Organic growth
- Daily improvement
- Faster response to changing conditions
- Innovation

In Lean management, process improvement (i.e. kaizen, see Note 4) is the *de facto* application of a theory of human development which enables an organization to adapt and respond rapidly to changing market conditions. It could also be described as a theory of human discontent with passivity and the status-quo, based on observation and causal analysis, informed by the need to for humans to survive. This can only be achieved by allowing people to think about their work and granting them freedom to improve their work without constantly needing to obtain management's permission. The habit for developing *de facto* reasoning is the application of the scientific method and its derivatives (see Notes 5 and 6).

The spiritual beliefs of executives trained in classical management exclude such excursions into the material realm. So, they must instead focus on gaining proficiency in other aspects of business leadership such as the ability to foretell the future.

Fortune-Telling

The mechanism by which a worker becomes a metaphysical leader, suffused with *de jure* reasoning, has now been illuminated. But, what benefit comes from that and for whom? Stated another way, who is the client and how do they derive advantage?

There are clear motivations based on social group (executive class) coherence and the advancement of the vested rights and interests of owners. But, to realize these benefits requires the support (or lack of resistance) of various stakeholders: employees, customers, suppliers, and investors. Each stakeholder has an interest in the continuing operations of the company, each stakeholder has a perspective, and each stakeholder has a need for information to help them understand past and current times, and, importantly, plan for the future.

As CEO, the metaphysical leader must process and present information for consumption by each stakeholder. Given that the past is the past, and the present is soon to be the past, the most important information conveyed by CEOs is about the future. The role of the top executive becomes that of a fortune-teller (see Note 6): one who makes predictions about the future of an organization (the company) or group of people (employees, suppliers, customer, investors, and communities).

To foretell the future with confidence, the CEO must learn how to prophesize credibly. This is a specialized skill, developed first as an apprentice fortune-teller, dutifully following the examples of leaders above, coupled with additional practice as one rises through the hierarchy. They also learn from failed or "dead" CEOs; leaders whose fortune-telling method, substance, style, or timing of prediction proved problematic to one's agenda or costly to one's job.

The prophecies conjured cast a spell on fellow executives and most employees, but typically not the workers who perform the actual work processes. Prophecies can vary greatly, from dark and foreboding to bright and providential. The common characteristics of prophecies from the CEOs of large corporations are summarized in Table 3-3:

Table 3-3: Common Characteristics of CEO Prophecies

Stakeholder	Characteristic	Reason
Employees	Dark, Ominous	Wage Freeze, Headcount Reduction
Suppliers	Dark, Ominous	Purchase Price Reduction (price squeeze)
Customers	Bright, Auspicious	Customer Satisfaction, Sales Growth
Investors	Bright, Auspicious	Earnings Growth, Stock Price
Communities	Dark, Ominous	Tax Reduction, Downsizing

Under standard conditions, anything that represents a cost is an ominous prophecy, while that which represent a gain is an auspicious prophecy. Under adverse conditions, all CEO prophecies turn dark (Gryta, 2018).

Prophecies take on many forms such as management exhortations:

- Failure is not an option
- Flawless execution
- Strengthen competitiveness
- Drive efficiency

They can be directed to foretell required conduct among managers:

- Budget (no variances)
- Schedule (no variances)

Foretell corporate performance:

- Growth forecasts
- Revenue forecasts
- Cash flow forecasts
- Earnings forecasts

And meet legal and fiduciary requirements:

- Quarterly government filings
- Proxy statements
- Annual report to shareholders

While the last category contains much information related to past business performance, it nevertheless establishes expectations for future performance. Financial reports, and especially the CEOs letter to shareholders, are examples of metaphysical statements – not experimentally testable (i.e. not independently replicable). As such, it requires people to have faith in documents as an accurate representation of the financial condition of a business. Faith is reinforced by using abstract words that convey senses of confidence, optimism, trust, inspiration, employee engagement, and the pursuit of new business opportunities. And one must have faith to believe in the predictions.

CEOs distance from the material realm (shop and office floor) means that all their time is spent experiencing the metaphysical realm. As the television show *Undercover Boss* proves time and time again (CBS, 2018), top leaders have no understanding of what actually happens in the material realm. Instead, they have abstract theories about what happens in the material realm – theories that are quickly and easily disproven when the top executive performs the job of a worker (or when they participate in kaizen). Possessing abstract or idealized theories of the work processes performed in the material realm pose a threat to corporate prosperity and survival (i.e. Veblen's mismanagement). This threat typically goes unrecognized by executives, while boards of directors welcome the spells cast by those who can skillfully foretell of fortunes.

Full commitment to the metaphysical realm and *de jure* reasoning are prized capabilities in the executive ranks and form the basis for defining one's honor. A previous study presented the details of characteristics that illuminate why it is very difficult for executives to return to *de facto* reasoning. In a nutshell, the progression of a business leader is from science to the metaphysical realm (Figure 3-2, left side), and often bordering on the theological (see Note 7).

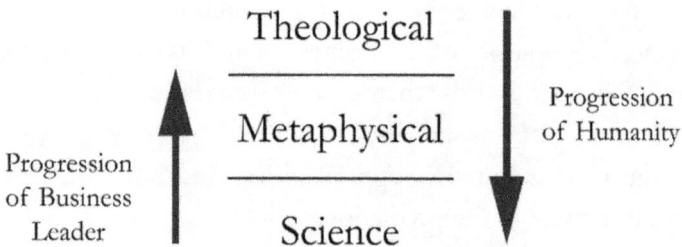

Figure 3-2. Stages of knowledge (right side) according to Auguste Comte (Comte, 1865). The progression of humanity is reversed (left side) in business when leaders abandon *de facto* reasoning in favor of *de jure* reasoning.

Returning to science from the metaphysical realm is seen as going backwards, and also constitutes an admission of having made a big mistake – not to mention the numerous poor and erroneous decision that were made in the past based on *de jure* reasoning. As a result, few executives will volunteer to re-engage the material realm.

However, it is not impossible to regenerate *de facto* reasoning in executives and sustain it over long periods of time. CEOs who decide to do this will likely find ample benefits and rewards.

Disrupting Classical Management Equilibrium

The combination of executive culture, politics suffused with archaic political economy, and metaphysical leadership create enduring equilibrium conditions that prevent management practice from evolving into modern times (Figure 3-3). The adoption of Lean management beyond its ineffective diluted forms is halted, except in those cases where the equilibrium can be successfully disrupted.

The question is, which force can be altered to disrupt the equilibrium? There are three candidates: Executive culture (F1), which is complex and interconnected. Politics and political economy (F2), which are entrenched and operate in the sphere of ideas and concepts that are difficult to displace based merit. That leaves F3, metaphysical leadership. Empirical evidence from successful Lean transformations reveals that metaphysical leadership, is the most favorable point of disruption.

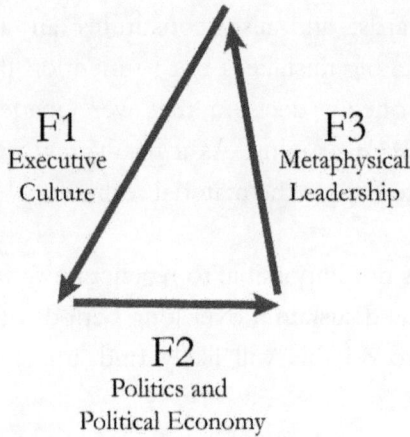

Figure 3-3. Vector diagram illustrating the forces of executive culture (F1), politics and political economy (F2), and metaphysical leadership (F3) which result in equilibrium and firm attachment to archaic management practices.

It is initiated by a change to the material leadership style: democratic, servant, or transformational (Table 3-2). This, of course, is not easy to do. But, if successful, it has the knock-on effect of significantly reducing politics and modifying political economy (F2) in ways that better align with the interests, perspectives, and information needs of employees, suppliers, customers, investors, and communities. It also alters executive culture in small yet meaningful ways that diminish the perceived value of status, honor, invidiousness, power, coercion, fealty, decorum, property, and ownership (though not necessarily wealth). In other words, material leadership is unifying.

Based on findings of Chapters 1, 2, and 3, the full focus and effort should be F3 – with a careful eye on F2, followed by F1, because opportunities for their modification will arise.

It is clear that separation between business leaders and workers and their work processes must be reduced. This, of course, is well known in Toyota, where even executives are required to maintain contact with genba, the workers and work processes, to improve observation skills and to assure managers understand the facts as well as cause-and-effect (Spear, 2004; Liker and Hoseus, 2008; Roser, 2017). This is fundamental to effectiveness as a material leader. Figure 3-4 shows that contact with the material realm is required throughout the management hierarchy.

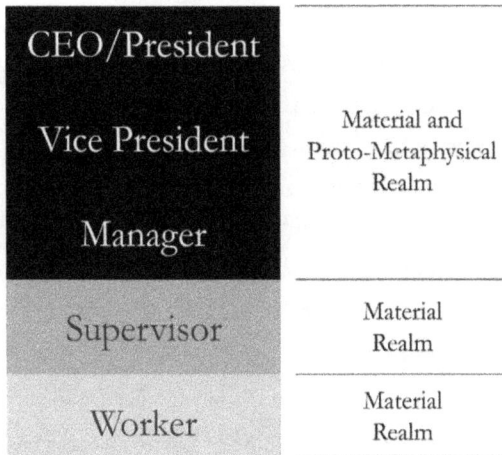

CEO/President	
Vice President	Material and Proto-Metaphysical Realm
Manager	
Supervisor	Material Realm
Worker	Material Realm

Figure 3-4. Maintaining contact with the material realm through successive advancement in organizations.

At the highest levels, the job demands contact with some of the metaphysical elements – no more contact than is necessary because it will change one's understanding of the work, produce more *de jure* than *de facto* reasoning, and thus distort information and information flows.

Periodic contact with the genba helps assure that preconceptions – wherever they may come from – do not solidify in the minds of executives; that dead ideas do not control executive reasoning so that individuals, organizations, society, and humanity can progress and survive (see Note 7).

Relatively simple changes to human resource policies for the promotion and evaluation processes for supervisors, managers, and executives are needed. The challenge will be in getting the CEO to see the need, and then sponsor the changes in these policies and processes to gain the approval of the board of directors. Obviously, policies must be enforced, and evaluation processes must be performed as required. And both must be continuously improved to incorporate new ideas and to reflect changing conditions. This will disrupt the equilibrium that has long existed in classical management and lead to needed changes in executive culture and their understanding of corporate politics and economics.

Recent demands for changes in corporate governance (e.g., Fink, 2018), coupled with incipient change-overs in generational leadership and the workforce, suggest that these changes might be more possible now than in the past. Perhaps it is through these coming changes that CEOs will see the need.

The material realm, shown in Table 3-4, is obviously generative, while the metaphysical leader's realm (Table 3-1) is characterized by individualism, distrust, misunderstandings, confrontation, and exploit – the type of corporate governance that creates malfeasance, expensive legal and corporate reputation problems, and the perpetual "lag, leak, and friction" that goes against the interests of all stakeholders.

Table 3-4: Material Leader's Realm

Material Element	Activity or Concern
Budget	Waste, Unevenness, Unreasonableness
Performance	Cost, Delivery, Quality, Safety
Labor	Listen, Help Workers, Trust, Respect
Location	Where Workers Work, Problem-Solving
Information Source	The Workplace (genba)
Communication	Language of Improvement / Evolution
Policies and Rules	Shared Interests
Domain of Supervision	People, Space, Process, Equipment
Allegiance	Company, Process, Learning
Personal Worth (status)	Teamwork, Ideas, Action, Know-How

The specialized skill of fortune-telling is largely replaced by practical visions, beliefs, and actions that are responsive to the interests of all stakeholders (e.g., Ballé, 2016; Toyoda, 2017). Realism and evolution are more highly prized than abstractions and stasis – which aligns with calls for improved corporate governance from investors as well as from employees. The pathway for doing better – for the CEO to perform at the high levels they expect from others

– is well known, eminently practical, and attainable through a cumulative series of small changes in mindset and routines.

Summary

Chapters 1, 2, and 3 have shown that the present-day management practice is permeated with the past (see Note 8), which results in man-made equilibrium conditions that prevent needed progress in the practice of management. Archaic business philosophy based on 18th and 19th century moral philosophy and political economy entrenches *de jure* reasoning and impedes the development and advancement of humans as well as business; it lowers the bar.

In Lean management, natural philosophy (i.e. natural liberty and natural rights), self-interest, laissez-faire, and unbridled profit-seeking take on different forms: earned liberty and earned rights, community, action, and profit-making through process improvement. The former pretends to advance business, but, in reality, it works to handicap business and impede progress, both for business and society. Lean management returns the pendulum to the normal condition.

Times have changed, and so it is necessary to clear out features of the past that prevent preparing for the future. But, the past will not go away by itself. Purposeful action must be taken to shed the past so that people and organizations can evolve. This can be done voluntarily, or it can be forced by rising discontent. CEOs constantly remind employees of their need evolve; to be proactive; to be engaged, to be innovative, to be adaptable, to be a problem-solver, to have empathy, and to continuously learn. Homiletical discourse has no meaning so along as CEOs continue to avoid their own good advice and signal their strong preference for maintaining equilibrium.

Assuring stasis is not meritorious work; it is improper, if not immoral. Persistent attachment to archaic habits of mind retard the necessary development and advancement of humans and their institutions. Rather than being something to avoid, transcendence from the metaphysical (*de jure*) realm to the material (*de facto*) realm must be recognized as an act of courageous leadership by forward-thinking CEOs, as well as a safe and sensible move. Material CEO's must replace metaphysical CEOs as the influential archetype to follow.

It seems likely that a majority of CEOs are very displeased with classical management due to its many limiting features (e.g. cold, uninspiring, slow, cumbersome, error- and defect-prone). Yet, executives fail to see how they inadvertently bring to fruition that which they dislike. This book has sought to illuminate how executives come to accept a situation that they have great antipathy towards but are forced to hide from others. The personal toll caused by the daily convulsion, clatter, and grind induced by the structural failings of classical management is not something that one should tolerate, whether for themselves or others.

Classical management is inhuman and unhealthy. It is an inept, unchanging creation which conforms to a metaphysical realm whose time has passed. There is no need to stick with it. Instead, leaders should experience a human-centered management system: Lean management (see Note 9).

Homework Assignment

1. Re-read Chapters 1, 2, and 3. Think deeply about what your read and answer this question in essay form: "What did I learn?" Consider your answers in relation to other things you have read or know about Lean management. Has progress been made? Are you now smarter and more capable of moving forward? How so?

2. Based on what you learned in Chapters 1, 2, and 3, create leader standard work for the senior executive team that reduces the separation between business leaders and workers and their work processes for a large corporation with distributed work sites. Step 1, document your preconceptions about leader standard work. Step 2, abandon those preconceptions. Step 3, reimagine leader standard work and create something new that senior executives can accept and will use. Think of five to seven unique methods for the new leader standard work practice. Each must be simple and low or no cost.

3. Create a dozen different visual controls (in multiple forms such as signs, symbols, physical objects, etc.) that will help top executives move from the metaphysical realm towards the material realm. What about audio controls? What about video controls?

4. The image on the following page depicts disruption of classical management equilibrium to move top executives from the metaphysical realm towards the material realm (F3). Identify several unique combinations of coercive actions and incentives that would aid the process of moving executives towards the material realm.

F1
Executive
Culture

F3
Metaphysical
Leadership

F2
Politics and
Political Economy

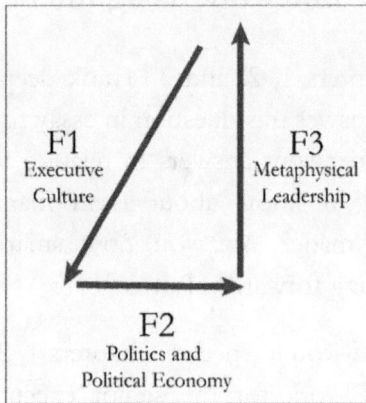

5. Once F3 is disrupted, what methods will you use to establish scientific method thinking among executives? Identity five methods for re-establishing the scientific method in executive's daily leadership and management practice.

6. Create practical processes for deploying the results of Notes 2, 3, 4, and 5, singly or in combination, with an eye towards developing social interaction among executives that influence one another to develop an interest in the material realm. Think of five to seven different processes. Each must be simple and low or no cost.

Notes

1. There are some notable successes of the adoption of Lean management in its full form. However, these examples are clearly the exception and not the rule. The rule is to adopt Lean management in diluted and distorted forms, or not at all.

2. The one area where conservative-minded executives have been remarkably progressive is in the rapid adoption of expensive analog and digital machine technologies to improve productivity and reduce labor costs – even in cases where humans can do the work with higher productivity and at lower cost. As Veblen says, the root of the conservative business leaders' *de jure* reasoning is money: "pecuniary premises to pecuniary conclusions" (Veblen, 1904, p. 320). In Lean management, *de facto* reasoning moderates or limits *de jure* reasoning and its effects on people and the enterprise. For example, machines (automation) are used only when the work is unsafe and when the quality specification cannot be achieved. This view reflects management's understanding of the worker and the work processes so that money is not wasted on efforts to improve productivity by indiscriminate purchase of expensive machines.

3. Lean management is distinct from Toyota's management system (Chapter 1, Figure 1-1). While the two share some similarities, they are different in numerous important ways (Monden, 1983; Ohno, 1988). Lean management and Toyota's management system are not synonymous.

4. Not all kaizen is the same. There are many variations of kaizen, most of which produce little or no business results. That's no good. Toyota-style kaizen is the baseline method to learn. It is rooted in industrial engineering methods, which anyone can learn, and utilizes people's ideas and creativity to rapidly improve processes without harming workers. See *Toyota Kaizen Methods: Six Steps to Improvement* by I. Kato and A. Smalley (2011); *Kaizen Forever: Teachings of Chihiro Nakao* by B. Emiliani, K. Yoshino, and R. Go, (2015); and *Shingijutsu-Kaizen: The Art of Discovery and Learning* by R. Wood, M. Herscher, and B. Emiliani (2015).

5. The scientific method is the baseline method used for *de facto* reasoning in Lean management. Derivatives of the scientific method used in Lean management include kaizen, plan-do-check-act cycle, root cause analysis (5 Whys and fishbone diagrams), and A3 reports.

6. There are numerous methods of fortune-telling including: astrology (fortune-telling by the movements of celestial bodies), extispicy (fortune-telling by the entrails of animals), nggàm (fortune-telling by actions of crabs or spiders), numerology (fortune-telling by numerical patterns). Business fortune-telling is called "pecuniology" (fortune-telling by money).

7. The past is ever-present. As a result, each of us has many more preconceptions than we realize. Notionally, the way you think is the sum of your age plus 100 years. For example, the moral philosopher and political economist Adam Smith was born in 1723. That means the core of his thinking, his preconceptions, come from 100 years earlier,

and are largely theological (i.e. "invisible hand;" the Creator) and metaphysical (Veblen, 1899, 1899a, 1900). It is unwise to rely on such reasoning 300 years later as if it produced a complete set immutable (natural) laws. It may be acceptable to possess such archaic views as an individual, but it is unacceptable to possess archaic views as a CEO who is responsible for the lives and livelihoods of thousands or tens of thousands of people. Just as we find no use for an unproductive 300-year-old machine, we should find no use for 300-year-old habits of mind that are likewise unproductive, and replace them with new productive habits of mind. We appreciate the work of those who came before us such as Adam Smith, and we are deeply influenced by them, but it is imperative that we think for ourselves based on our own observation and experiences in the material realm.

8. Thorstein Veblen identified preconceptions in economic science (Veblen, 1899a, p. 407-414) used by earlier schools of economic thought. The economic preconceptions of the Physiocrats (18th century French economists) were rooted in the productiveness of nature – the "nutritive process of Nature" – and the owners of agricultural lands. Later, Adam Smith, whose book, *The Wealth of Nations* (1776) inaugurated the start of classical economics, operated under the economic preconceptions of human labor in handicraft and agriculture, guided by "the natural course" (design by God; divine order). The "undevout utilitarians" soon gave rise to hedonistic "economic man" as one's purpose. The economic preconceptions of business leaders (as well as political leaders), from the industrial revolution, to the machine age, to the second industrial revolution, and into

the atomic, jet, and digital ages, have remained much the same as Adam Smith's. The continued attachment to archaic economic preconceptions in the information age and beyond could prove to be calamitous.

9. As indicated in Note 3, Lean management is not the same as Toyota's management system. The latter more fully-features humanism than the former.

References

Ballé, M., (2016), "Is There a Spiritual Dimension to Lean?", *Lean Enterprise Institute*, 7 November, https://www.lean.org/balle/DisplayObject.cfm?o=3330, accessed 13 January 2018

CBS   (2018),   "Undercover   Boss," http://www.cbs.com/shows/undercover_boss/,   *CBS Television*, accessed 17 January 2018. See also https://en.wikipedia.org/wiki/ Undercover_ Boss

Comte, A. (1865), Bridges, J.H. (translator), *A General View of Positivism*, Trubner and Co., London, U.K. Reissued by Cambridge University Press, 2009

Eagly, Alice H. and Johannesen-Schmidt, Mary C. (2001), "The Leadership Styles of Women and Men," *Journal of Social Issues*, Vol. 57, No. 4, pp. 781-797, http://dx.doi.org/10.1111/0022-4537.00241, accessed 16 January 2018

Emiliani, B., Stec., D., Grasso, L., and Stodder, J. (2007), *Better Thinking, Better Results: Case Study and Analysis of an Enterprise-Wide Lean Transformation*, The CLBM, LLC, Wethersfield, Conn.

Emiliani, B. (2015), *Speed Leadership: A New Way to Lead for Rapidly Changing Times*, The CLBM, LLC, Wethersfield, Conn.

Fink, L. (2018), "A Sense of Purpose," Larry's Fink's 2018 Letter to CEOs, 17 January, *Blackrock Inc.*, https://www.blackrock.com/corporate/en-us/investor-relations/larry-fink-ceo-letter, accessed 17 January 2018

Gryta, T. (2018), "Troubles Push GE to Consider a Breakup," *The Wall Street Journal*, 16 January, https://www.wsj.com/articles/ge-expects-6-2-billion-charge-after-reviewing-insurance-reserve-1516104171, accessed 16 January 2018

Koskela, L. and Kagioglou, M. (2006), "On the Metaphysics of Lean Management," 14th Annual Conference of the International Group for Lean Construction, 25-27 July, Ponteficia Universidad Católica de Chile, Santiago, Chile, http://usir.salford.ac.uk/9368/, accessed 17 January 2018

Liker, J. and Hoseus, M. (2008), *Toyota Culture, The Heart and Soul of The Toyota Way*, McGraw-Hill Education, New York, NY

Ohno, T. (1988), *Toyota Production System – Beyond Large-Scale Production*, Productivity Press, Portland, OR

Person, H. (Ed.) in Taylor, F.W. (1947), *Scientific Management: Comprising Shop Management, Principles of Scientific Management, Testimony Before the House Committee*, H. Person, Ed., Harper & Brothers Publishers, New York, NY, p. xii

Roser, C. (2017), "The Toyota Employee Evaluation System," *All About Lean*, 26 December, http://www.allaboutlean.com/toyota-employee-evaluation/, accessed 14 January 2018

Spear, S. (2004), "Learning to Lead at Toyota," *Harvard Business Review*, May, Vol. 82, No. 5, pp. 78-86

Stone, D. (1989), "Causal Stories and the Formation of Political Agendas," *Political Science Quarterly*, Vol. 104, No. 2, pp. 281-300

Toyoda, A. (2017), "Making Ever-better Cars and Human Resource Development: The Forces That Power Sustainable Growth," Message from the President, October, http://www.toyota-global.com/company/message_from_president/, accessed 16 January 2018

Veblen, T. (1899), "The Preconceptions of Economic Science I," *The Quarterly Journal of Economics*, Vol. 13, No. 2, January, pp. 121-150

Veblen, T. (1899a), "The Preconceptions of Economic Science II," *The Quarterly Journal of Economics*, Vol. 13, No. 4, July, pp. 396-426

Veblen, T. (1900), "The Preconceptions of Economic Science III," *The Quarterly Journal of Economics*, Vol. 14, No. 2, February, pp. 240-269

Veblen, T. (1904), *The Theory of Business Enterprise*, Charles Scribner's Sons, New York, NY

Veblen, T. (1914), *The Instinct of Workmanship: And the State of the Industrial Arts*, The Macmillan Company, New York, NY
Veblen, T. (1921), *The Engineers and the Price System*, B.W. Huebsch, Inc., New York, NY

Womack, J.P. (2017), "Jim Womack on Where Lean Has Failed and Why Not to Give Up," *Planet Lean: The Lean Global Network Journal*, 29 August, http://planet-lean.com/jim-womack-on-where-lean-has-failed-and-why-not-to-give-up, accessed 14 January 2018

4

Dismantling Classical Management

Abstract

The common and long-standing way in which businesses are managed, classical management, is based on moral and economic philosophies dating to the 18th and 19th centuries, and earlier. Classical management is thus rooted in these and other strong, long-lived traditions that make it hostile to improvement as times change. The 21st century times we now live in, coupled with the challenges that business and humanity face, demand improved management practice. Small adjustments to the basic structure and practice of classical management have long been made, yet they invariably lag far behind the time they are needed. Furthermore, additional fine-tuning of a largely static, outdated management method is no longer sufficient. The entrenchment of classical management suggests that it is unlikely to be replaced on a large scale by using conventional means such as training and education. Therefore, more forceful processes must be established to dismantle classical management, with the goal of replacing it with a modern, dynamic, continuously adaptable management method that serves the needs of business and humanity now and in the future. This chapter examines four novel approaches to dismantling classical management based on the following grounds: public health policy, duty of care, antitrust, and constitutionality.

Note: This chapter explores the research question: If classical management could be dismantled, how would you do it?

Introduction

Classical management is the management method commonly used in all types of organizations – for profit, not-for-profit, government, and non-governmental organizations – regardless of the organizations' purpose or their customers' needs. It is the conjoining of numerous sub-processes which collectively are applied to assemble and coordinate people, material, information, and other resources to achieve vital objectives. Fundamental to the proper execution of classical management is hierarchical structure, servile manager-worker relationships, coercive superintendence of work and of workers, batch-and-queue processing of material and information (see Note 1), production scale and sales growth dicta, the use of expediency and leverage to achieve temporal goals and objectives, predatory and bellicose market-facing behaviors, to name a few (see Note 2). It should be obvious that this combination of characteristics produces a strong commitment, if not overcommitment, to results (see Note 3), and corresponding inattention to processes and their details.

Classical management is viewed as the consensus best management practice, both right and good, and precisely aligned with leaders' responsibilities fulfill the organization's mission and assure survival. It is accepted by generations of business leaders, politicians, educators, journalists, and others as having few major faults, and is considered superior to any other competing management method. Classical management is therefore implicitly judged to be an unimpeachable incumbent fully capable of keeping up with changing times as business progresses from the 18th century industrial revolution through to 21st century information age, and therefore in no need of major revision despite changing times and needs. While there have been numerous attempts to improve management practice, they invariably fail to influence the broader practice of classical management (see Note 4). Classical management thus remains the default management method for both capitalist and non-capitalist enterprises.

The origins of classical management date back to 18th and 19th century moral and economic philosophy informed by animism. These "handicraft era" foundations remain more-or-less in place, while some elements pre-date this era, such as ancient administration of the polity (BC era), English common law (ca. 1100 AD), and the balance sheet (ca. 1500) (Figure 4-1). Classical management has endured despite being formulated on ideas and assumptions that were sensible for the times in which they were established. These traditions are carried forward, largely uncritically, by various means such as: coaching and mentoring, work experience, on-the-job training, journalism, and undergraduate and graduate education. Additionally, leaders have at their disposal legions of peers who can provide trustworthy advice and counsel based on a common understanding of classical management thinking and practice. Classroom learning, as well as company-sponsored training, is no match for the social learning that occurs on-the-job; it is the most powerful for perpetuating antiquated traditions and wisdom.

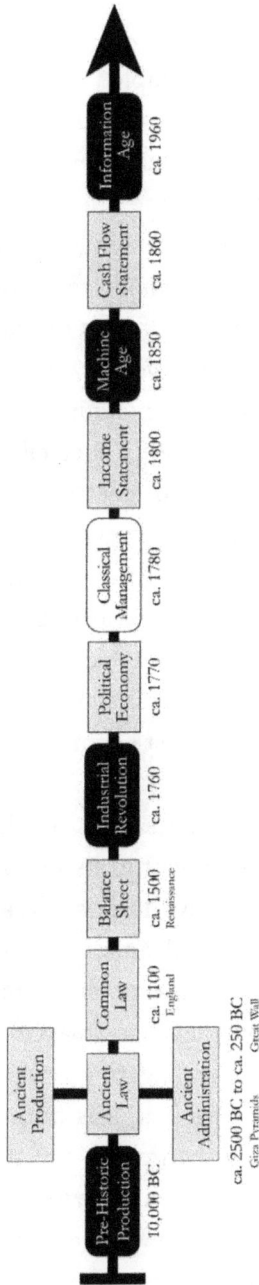

Figure 4-1. Illustration of key elements that led to the creation of classical management, transmitted from the past to the present.

The passing of time, coupled with uncritical acceptance, has made classical management the cornerstone of "common sense" of business management. It is seen to have withstood the test of time, therefore earning its place as the default mode of management, and thus obviating the need for leaders to fundamentally re-examine it or break from it in search of progressive forms of management (see Note 5). By many measures, classical management has worked well in generating the expected benefits – growth in gross domestic product, wealth creation, societal prosperity, greater life expectancy, and so on. Yet these are past successes, and past successes are no guarantee of future success – especially given that the future is destined to be so unlike the past. The many preconceptions associated with past success effectively disable broad-based critical re-examinations of the utility and effectiveness of classical management for the 21st century and beyond.

If everyone thinks the same way about management, then there is no improvement in its philosophy or practice. As a result, it fails to evolve in positive and balanced ways over time. Knowledge advances when preconceptions are challenged on their face or facilitated by the emergence of new information or changing circumstances. One must identify a substantial lingering problem and envision a new definition of success. Yet, it is not in the remit of leaders – business leaders in particular – to make unfamiliar changes whose outcomes are uncertain, based upon their prior personal experience. They are expected to do what is known from prior experience (self or others) to yield favorable results. There are numerous economic, social, political, historical, and philosophical preconceptions in classical management, few of which are ever challenged by leaders. It is a much easier and smoother path for them to accept rather than critique or reject. The consequence is a voluntary drought of new ideas for improving the practice of management in the information age.

Any person in a leadership position should possess the same basic mindset: "We can do better." Meaning, a mindset that challenges the "common sense" of classical management in search of a new critically-derived "good sense" of management. It is a mindset conjoined with practical actions that continuously seeks better ways of doing things to yield better results as circumstances continuously change. This dynamic, evolving mindset is not just for producing better business results (achieving strategies goals, and objectives), but also for the practice of management itself and associated leadership routines. Because this does not typically happen with classical management, it is apparent that the usefulness of classical management becomes continuously and deliberately reduced over time. Unthinking adherence to traditions and preconceptions, produced by a static mindset, has crippled classical management to the point that it has outlived its usefulness. Classical management is obsolete. Business and society, which must progress forward, can ill afford the continued widespread use of an antiquated management method. Business leaders who desire to preserve a relic of the past do so for their own benefit.

There should be no doubt, however, that classical management will not be easily displaced, as there is too great a personal investment in it (see Note 6), and that investment extends globally and to any organization that incorporates professional managers. It also includes investments by equity trading markets, regulators, courts, legislators, and other parties. Classical management is deeply entrenched, and therefore few leaders will voluntarily give up classical management and replace it with a progressive management method which embodies the engineering mindset of rapid experimentation and the use of the scientific method (see Notes 7 and 8). The conspicuous methods for displacing classical management, such as benchmarking (performance data and company visits), persuasion (logical arguments), changes to public and private education (curriculum), and corporate training (classroom and on-the-job), will produce only minor, and assuredly inconsistent, results. Nevertheless, these methods have some value and should not be abandoned.

Because the possibility of displacing classical management on a large scale using conventional thinking and practices is remote, the better strategy is to dismantle it through more forceful processes such as public policy, health risk litigation, trade and commerce legislation, and legal challenges to its legitimacy – likely all four (see Note 9). If successful, this would forcibly break long-established traditions and preconceptions, and begin the process of robust competition for new, modern progressive forms of management practice that are more fit for current and future times, with the intent of generating broader-based benefits than classical management can deliver, while working continuously to make adjustments that minimize expected or known deficiencies. Static leadership mindsets and static management methods would give way to dynamic leadership mindsets and dynamic management methods in the fast-moving digital era (Emiliani, 2015).

While this Introduction highlighted organizations in general, subsequent pages feature one type of organization: for-profit business. Profit-seeking businesses make full use of the 18th and 19th century moral and economic grounds on which classical management is based – as well as its enlargement and extension of these grounds to expand profit-seeking opportunities whose outcomes are most often zero-sum. The gain by business at the expense of other stakeholders, such as employees, suppliers, or communities, has long been a signifying characteristic of classical management. As such, the profit-seeking business application of classical management more fully reveals the extent of its deficiencies and underscores the pressing need for its replacement with a better and more sustainable profit-seeking management method.

This chapter examines four novel approaches to dismantling classical management based on the following grounds: public health policy, duty of care, antitrust, and constitutionality. Namely, classical management as a public health hazard and resulting epidemic; the obligation by natural or legal persons to adhere to a rational and sensible standard of care when performing acts that can foreseeably cause harm to others; classical management as a necessary and integral component of business leaders' efforts reduces competition and controls markets and pricing; and classical management as unconstitutional based on the 5th and 9th amendments of the U.S. Constitution. Namely, deprivation of life, liberty, and due process, unenumerated rights (i.e.

implied or fundamental rights), and the commerce clause. It is postulated that progressive forms of management would be better positioned to compete for adoption by business leaders if classical management were rendered less powerful and made substantially less useful through these actions. While the focus of the chapter is the United States and U.S. law, it is thought that similar arguments can be made in other countries.

Public Health Policy

Public health is nominally defined as protecting the safety and health of human communities through science, education, and policy. A public health hazard is nominally defined as a condition known to be hazardous to humans through long-term (greater than one year) exposure. Employers, whether they are publicly-traded or privately held business, draw employees from the public sphere. Specific jobs held by employees can themselves be hazardous, or groups of employees could be exposed to hazardous environments. The context for job-related hazards are typically substances or equipment in-use, but it also extends to management practice if it places the general population of employees into a state of ill physical or mental health. This can be caused by the management practice itself, inclusive of associated leadership routines, the presence of sociopathic managers, or both.

Recall the signifying characteristics of classical management: hierarchical structure, servile manager-worker relationships, coercive superintendence of work and of workers, batch-and-queue processing of material and information, production scale and sales growth dicta, the use of expediency and leverage to achieve temporal goals and objectives (Boston, 2018), predatory and bellicose market-facing behaviors, and zero-sum outcomes. It is stating the obvious to say that classical management is more welcoming to sociopathic leaders and managers whose shared pattern of behavior is to blame people for problems (a strong form of oppressive and coercive power and control), which stifles employees' creativity and disables their ability to generate new ideas. That, coupled with the signifying characteristics, render classical management to be a poor method of management. By its very design, this method of assembling and coordinating people, material, information, and other resources is heavily burdened with structural deficiencies that cause both people and processes to underperform.

The long-settled leadership mindset in classical management is to subject employees to various types of poor treatment, more or less, throughout the range of practice, aided by the aggressive and often ill-considered introduction of new technologies that displace employees. The net effect is to confuse and create ambiguity in one's standing, while impairing the ability to perform work processes expertly and efficiently, and thus obtain favorable performance reviews from supervisors (see Note 10). These factors, and the never-ending threats listed below, combine to expose the general population of employees to the long-term health hazard of chronic stress (Goh et al., 2016).

- Layoffs
- Offshoring

- Outsourcing
- Computers, software, and automation
- Business performance metrics
- Organizational politics
- Department reorganizations
- Frequent changes in owners, leaders, or managers

Expediency, as one of the primary modes of executive decision-making exercised in search of profits, renders these threats as ever-present to employees. These threats lie beyond mere marketplace dynamics and the need to earn profit to assure survival. They exist as part of routines commonly applied by business leaders for the purpose of maximizing pecuniary gains for owners and investors along short-term time horizons – one of many measures of business success that do not align with employees' core career and material interests. The threatening environment is obvious to virtually all employees (see Note 11), whether they are employed by publicly-traded or privately held business. Yet, employees are unaware of how these constant threat effects their physical and mental health and well-being.

Business leaders are fond of saying "There is no free lunch." Yet, they selectively, if not willingly, ignore the connection between classical management and human health, while simultaneously decrying the high cost of healthcare for employees. In other words, the effect of poor management, one that generates chronic stress in some or all of the employee population, is judged by leaders to be inconsequential to both employee health and business interests. In hierarchical organizations, those at the top consider themselves to be more valuable, more worthy, and more deserving than the general population of non-executive managers and employees. In the common executive view, these socioeconomically unsuccessful employees exist as an out-group, considered, to varying degrees, as untrustworthy, incompetent, unresponsive, unfit to provide meaningful feedback or analysis, and lacking competency for involvement in management decision-making. These and similar stigma legitimize and institutionalize poor management practices and associated leadership routines. Over time, this creates socioeconomic conditions that are judged by insiders (business leaders, investors, employees) and outsiders (politicians, educators, journalists) to be a both normal and acceptable, when, in fact, it is unacceptable and abnormal (Sapolsky, 2018).

In the United States, there are presently some 125 million full-time and 27 million part-time workers. Assuredly, some measurable, if not significant fraction of full- and part-time workers are not subject to conditions that produce chronic stress, or they are psychologically and physiologically more able to adapt. But it is also certain that many tens of millions are subject to chronic stress, given the ubiquity of classical Management, that is beyond the average employees' ability to adapt, which renders it a public health hazard of sufficient magnitude to be termed an epidemic. An "epidemic" is traditionally understood to be a disease, principally a physical ailment, that spreads quickly among a population or community. The effects of chronic stress are both physical and mental, are less visible, and spread slowly, though it is no less a hazard to human health than influenza or opioid epidemics.

Acute stress has always been, and will always be, part of business, because employees must periodically respond quickly to sudden or unanticipated business problems. The concern is when high stress levels become part of employees' everyday work environment. We can either ignore the problem and say, "That's just the way things are," or we be curious and can commit the resources to connect cause-and-effect through detailed analysis and controlled study. For decades, the effect of chronic stress on employee health and wellness were largely ignored by those who possessed the job and training to study such matters: management professors and health researchers. In the last two decades or so, research has brought the numerous ill effects of chronic stress into clear focus (Heminway, 2008; Pfeffer, 2018).

Chronic stress results in the continuous release of high levels of stress hormones, glucocorticoids (a class of steroid hormone) and epinephrine (adrenaline), into the blood stream. This accelerates the aging process and slowly kills people. The resulting medical problems, both physical and mental, include:

- Atherosclerosis
- Hypertension
- Visceral (belly) fat
- Chromosome damage (rapid aging via telomere unravelling)

- Weakened immune system
- Hippocampal atrophy (reduced learning and memory)
- Neuron (nerve cell) damage
- Fear and anxiety
- Depression
- Poor nutrition
- Inactivity (lack of exercise)

Importantly, these problems, which amount to a re-modeling of the human body, will typically occur in combination with one another, leading to intensification of overall poor health as time progresses. Importantly, chronic stress also affects the human body in ways that are passed on via reproduction to the next generation (Landhuis, 2018).

In the United States, most of the workforce is employed under a contractual relationship known as "at-will" employment. This means that employees can be dismissed by their employer for any reason, at any time, and with no warning, provided that no laws were violated. An adult person between the ages of 18 and 65 cannot reasonably live in America without employment as it lacks social safety nets for both basic income and healthcare. So, employed persons, especially those with dependents, have much to worry about, every day and every night, between the travails of work and life in the 21st century.

Employees, drawn from the public sphere, cannot be held accountable for their inability to deflect the slow but steady influx of physical and mental debilitation given that workplace conditions under classical management are intrinsically non-adaptable for some. Employees' long-term exposure to chronic stress resulting from the regular functioning of classical management by business leaders constitutes a real and present public health hazard. The antidote is not stress management classes and the like, for they fail to address the fundamental source of what induces employee illness. The chronic stress epidemic in the workplace requires public health policy solutions to guide legislative actions that reduce the public health hazard (Stone, 1989), and, importantly, constant monitoring and adjustment to correct imperfect ideation, planning, and decision-making. The form and shape of public policy and legislation must include the relevant stakeholders: business, government, healthcare, and labor, at minimum.

Duty of Care

In civil litigation, "duty of care" is a legal construct that requires a natural or legal person (i.e. the corporation via "personhood") to conduct affairs that could be foreseen to harm others with a reasonable standard of care. The previous section explicated how classical management, as actualized in practice by managers, is structurally deficient with respect to its effect on human health and well-being. Therefore, classical management can be foreseen to cause harm to other persons – employees as well as the corporation. In this way, corporate leaders and board of directors fail in their duty of care obligation under the law and can be claimed to be negligent by employees as well as shareholders.

Employees, under the day-by-day, if not hour-by-hour supervision and control of management, place at least one-third of their life and their livelihood into the hands of others above them. Managers either accept or reject that responsibility. In classical management, that responsibility is mostly rejected, by design. Yet, the implied social contract between employer and employee does not include any provision for employees having to endure work environments that result in long-term physical or mental deterioration. The employee claimant, as an individual or class, can pursue a claim of negligence resulting in legal liability to the corporation (past as well as present) and seek redress in the form of specific changes in management practice, financial compensation, or both. It could also include external monitoring by a third party to assure compliance with the terms of redress.

The employee class would have to produce evidence of injury, which could be accomplished through analysis personal medical records. Alternatively, or in tandem with personal medical records, the discovery process would allow inquiry and analysis of corporate medical data to identify health trends in the employee population over time to differentiate the normal aging process from health problems caused by long-term exposure to chronic stress in the workplace. This would establish the magnitude and certainty of injury, as well as the connection to the defendant's conduct (accountability). It should be relatively easy to prove that the conduct was useful to the defendant (e.g. to achieve assigned business targets to receive a bonus, stock options, or other special compensation), precautions were not taken, that alternative conduct is both feasible, practical, and useful in the pursuit of business, and that alternative conduct is not costly nor is it a burden to managers or unsafe. Successful litigation would prove that duty of care has been breached (see Note 12), thereby exposing the corporation, the board of directors, and likely individual managers (or perhaps nearly the entire senior management team), to liability and consequent redress.

Given the ubiquity of classical management, it would seem that a large number of corporations, particularly large corporations, may be exposed to legal action. This could prove costly for them both with respect to protracted legal defense and the possibility of substantial financial compensation to injured parties or their dependents. Adherents to classical management would be wise to consider their predicament as akin to the harm to human health cause by cigarette makers. Tobacco plaintiffs' template for successful litigation may be a useful guide and could result in the awarding of large punitive damages.

In recent times, many large corporations have adopted various elements of progressive management, and they may be given some credit for that. Yet, most, if not nearly all, have failed to substantially replace classical management with something better. For decades, corporate leaders have resisted external and internal calls for change to progressive management, for a panoply of reasons that are now clear. Therefore, the management practice in use today is largely unchanged (Gryta and Mann, 2018), which consequently has done little to ameliorate chronic stress work environments. As a result, millions of employees remain exposed to chronic stress. Human health is not an individualized manager value resting on differential moral foundations or traditions.

It is within reason to question the attentiveness and prudence of managers in the conduct of their duties, including their supervisory and decision-making functions, and whether these have been carried out in good faith when practical alternatives are commonly known and have been available to them for decades. It is doubtful that managers have acted in the full interest of the corporation, its shareholders, and relevant other stakeholders. Business leaders may want to think about proactively adopting the following vision and the management methods that can help achieve it: "We, the leaders of the corporation, will create a workplace that improves human physical and mental health, with the aim of employees leaving work every day in better health than when they arrived."

Antitrust

Because business is nominally based on prices generated by free markets (the "price system," Veblen, 1904, 1921), the easiest way to gain control over prices is monopoly, oligopoly, restrict output, collusion between industry participants (Abelson, 2018; Kendall, 2018; Mathews, 2018; Rowland, 2018), patents, or innovative new products or services – generally, commonly in that order. Overall, any one of these are easy to achieve within the framework of classical management to gain temporary or long-term control of prices. The most that might be required is to spend money to purchase the sought-after advantage. In simple terms, the overwhelming preference among CEOs is to find easy ways to business success (profits) and retain advantages, largely unchanged, for as long as possible (Thiel, 2014; Buffett 2017). Classical management is less interested in vigorously competing in the marketplace, and more interested in gaining various forms of restful differential advantage. Business leaders seek to create sellers' markets wherever possible, and by various means, because it greatly simplifies their duty to create wealth for owners and investors – whose knock-on effects include the concentration of private wealth and economic and political control (Wu, 2018) in ways that can cause harm to individuals, society, and its institutions. This feature is built into classical management, via its 18th and 19th century moral and economic philosophical grounds, beginning with Natural Rights (see Note 13).

As a direct descendant of medieval European feudalism, classical management embodies many characteristics that favor individual pursuits such as self-aggrandizement (careerism) and aggressive efforts to build personal wealth. It is very successful at attracting like-minded persons. To achieve those ends, leaders commonly engage in practices such as misrepresentation (lying), subterfuge (cheating), dispossession and expropriation (stealing) in pursuit of wealth creation. When malfeasance is exposed, leaders' public responses follow a similar pattern: silence, followed by misdirection, chicanery, prevarication, and hypocrisy in a concerted effort to make intentions or actions difficult to legally prove. Ultimately, there is a confluence of business interests (create sellers' markets) and personal interests (wealth) that is facilitated by classical management, which is directly linked to the seeking of higher prices.

This brief outline of common characteristics of business activity illustrates that competition is something that most business leaders would prefer to avoid. Said another way, business leaders cannot be trusted to engage in fair competition. Instead, they seek to make long-term structural changes in the marketplace to reduce competition (mergers, acquisitions, vertical combinations) and process changes (restrict output, contracts, tying, predatory pricing, collusion) that harm consumer welfare in the short-term (Khan, 2017; 2018). The overall purpose is to gain pricing power, which exposes such actions to state and federal antitrust scrutiny and possible enforcement. For all their boisterous heralding of free markets, business leaders are surprisingly anti-competition, because they recognize that competing in free markets is incredibly difficult. The easier path is to restrain trade via manipulation of price and output. Relatedly, large companies regularly seek to use their buying power extract price concessions from suppliers (squeeze suppliers, both large and small; i.e. monopsony), thus impinging upon fair trade. The common, though not inevitable, result is higher consumer prices with essentially no improvement in corporate operating efficiency, continued low productivity growth, underperforming economies, and periods of economic stagnation.

Current antitrust legislation, produced by attorneys with substantial help from leading economists, indicates that the competitive process itself – and hence economic efficiency, whether among many or few players – is poorly understood at the macro-level of the economy and especially at the micro-level of the company (see Note 14). Therefore, antitrust laws and enforcement actions are forced to focus on results and ignore the processes that generate antitrust problems. As a result, it is blind to any differences in management method and embedded production or other methods used in the concatenated processes that create value for customers (i.e. marketing, design, production, distribution, sales, aftermarket, etc.). Broadly, productive methods, whether in manufacturing or knowledge work, can be classified as batch-and-queue and flow. The former is the production method attached to classical management practice, while the latter, flow, is an integral feature of modern progressive management practice. The efficiency of batch-and-queue is inferior to that of flow by one-half or more – in an activity, business, where a just few points can create a huge differential in performance. To assume there are no great differences in management method or in the efficiency of production methods is tantamount to malpractice by lawyers and economists – people who serve as key determinants of citizens' life, liberty, and happiness. Process matters, and, of course, so do results.

Given the choice between batch-and queue or flow, one would expect business leaders to immediately choose the most efficient production method, flow. However, flow does not allow managers to manipulate price and output easily (i.e. throttling supply to affect demand and prices), and so batch-and-queue is the preferred method. Additionally, batch-and-queue is efficient only at scale (Figure 4-2), which embodies large capital requirements, and thus presents formidable barriers to market entry by potential competitors (entrepreneurs). Scale, which invites "the curse of bigness," often leads to overproduction, to absorb overhead costs, which generates tempting opportunities to substantially lower prices and place pressure on smaller competitors with furtive intent to drive them out of business. Finally, market forces are unable to function correctly and punish companies employing the less efficient batch-and-queue production method if most or all companies are using it – especially in highly concentrated markets. The result is that there is no incentive for business leaders to abandon classical management and its associated inefficient methods of manufacturing or service production. The switch to progressive management and its far more efficient methods of production is not something that most business leaders would voluntarily undertake (see Note 15).

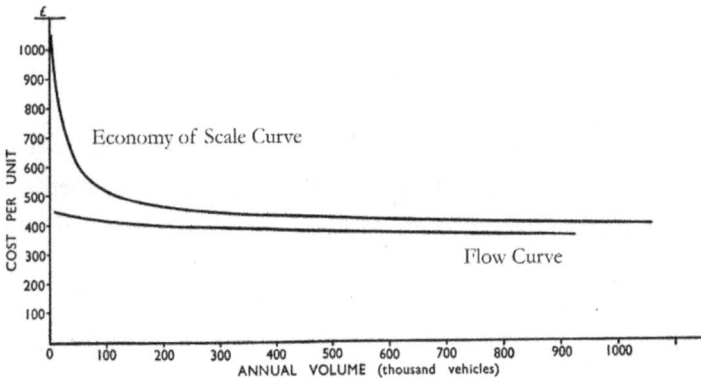

Figure 4-2. Classic economy of scale curve (batch-and-queue) compared to the flow curve. It immediately apparent that flow is the far more efficient method of production. The flow curve shows that the cost-volume dependence is weak when set-up time, queue time, and transportation time are greatly reduced (from days or hours to minutes or seconds). Lawyers and economists incorrectly assume only one production method (batch-and-queue) and time independence (adapted from Maxcy and Silberston, 1954).

Fundamentally, classical management and progressive management are resource administration architectures (RAAs) whose efficiency determines the wealth of individuals (workers and managers), companies (shareholders), and nations (society). The efficiency of the former is inherently low due to the abundance of queues and large capital needs, so costs are inherently high (and therefore prices). This drains funds from the research and development and related activities needed to produce innovative new products and services, thereby restraining the advancement of both national and consumer interests. It also holds down wages and salaries and thus consumer spending. Remarkably, neither antitrust law nor antitrust enforcement actions recognize the role of the management method in leaders' pursuit of anticompetitive structural and process changes, and its still-robust connection to 18th and 19th century moral and economic philosophies (Veblen, 1904). The management method (and production method) is not seen as part of any antitrust problem, when, in fact, they are inseparable.

Successful antitrust enforcement requires corporations to reverse the harm caused by management's anticompetitive actions. Concomitant with that, it could also require the dismantling of the management method that helped produce it − classical management − and require the institution of reforms consistent with the practical scope and aims of progressive management. This ties together the idea that there can be a concentration of power in markets as well as a concentration of power in the management method used by corporations, both of which are necessary to produce anticompetitive behavior. Market concentration, and concomitant reduction in competition, then leads to even deeper entrenchment of classical management, thus illustrating their synergistic workings.

But why wait for harm to be done to the marketplace and consumer welfare? The switch to progressive management would be a low-cost preventative measure to avoid anticompetitive actions and government scrutiny. Boards of directors could require a transition from classical to progressive management to help assure both the integrity of the business and public trust, and to avoid allegations (and the costs) of anticompetitive behavior. Government could mandate or incentivize a transition to progressive management to promote more vigorous marketplace competition with the aim of creating a healthier free market that enhances consumer welfare (greater variety, innovation, lower prices, better quality, availability) and reduces the size and cost government bureaucracy.

Progressive forms of management practice are less bound to 18th and 19th century moral and economic philosophy. They have at their foundation strong interest to vigorously compete in free markets, and they encumber themselves with a far more difficult challenge than the mere spending of money: Charge market or higher prices by delivering greater value to customers. This requires different management processes that impel a deeper understanding of customer wants and needs, as these change continuously over time. They enjoy the many challenges that stem from buyers' markets. In short, processes embedded in progressive management demand that all employees continuously observe, think, and rapidly experiment to retain a dynamic, rather than static, footing that is responsive to changes in customer needs and market conditions.

Fundamental to the proper execution of progressive management is hierarchical structure, yet the manager-worker relationship is one of mentoring and coaching focused on problem recognition and the application of problem-solving routines, and rather than coercive superintendence of work and of workers, employees are taught to think about their work every day and generate many ideas on how to improve it, and work together in teams. The method of processing material and information is flow, not batch-and-queue, and so the need for scale is reduced, while market share and sales growth are the result of superior capabilities to satisfy customer wants and needs. The scientific method and its derivatives are faithfully applied to recognize and correct problems, rather than expediency or leverage, and so processes are blamed, not people, when problems arise. Supplier- and customer-facing behaviors are cooperative and designed to result in mutual gain (vs. leverage), and thus not predatory and bellicose. Progressive management largely rejects the signifying characteristics of classical management, thereby revealing the focus of its many improvements over classical management – in particular, customer focus, human relations (employees and suppliers) and the ability to respond rapidly to unpredictable market conditions. It should be obvious that this combination of characteristics produces a process-focused management practice that is designed to yield consistently beneficial results.

True believers in free markets, if they actually exist, should eagerly support the dismantling of classical management. They should want to let competition do its job, as is commonly imagined. The competitive process, made up of many participants, practical rules for fair play, and conspicuous punishments, should be freed from the shackles of classical management.

Constitutionality

The three previous sections have highlighted the harms caused by the ubiquitous use of classical management in business: public health policy, duty of care, and antitrust. Through the Constitution of the United States of America (as amended) (Jefferson et al., 1788), the federal government has a legal responsibility to promote the general welfare of the people. The health hazards caused by chronic stress are at odds with the general welfare of the people. There is also a requirement to promote the progress of science and regulate commerce. Taken together, these could be grounds for arguing that classical management infringes on the constitutional rights of the people (natural persons, employees and dependents, in the range of some 200+ million people) based on:

- The Fifth Amendment, deprivation of life and liberty (equal protection principles)
- The Fifth Amendment, violation of due process
- The Ninth Amendment, unenumerated rights reserved to the people

Violation of due process takes the indirect form of government inaction that harms life and liberty by the failure to recognize the ill effects to people and to commerce caused by the classical management method, and its impact on future generations (posterity) (see Note 13). The country's future prosperity and public welfare is placed at risk through the inability of the people to work on terms that minimize hazards that result in the degradation of human health. The U.S. government has failed to recognize and protect the people's fundamental rights to life and liberty in this regard. Additionally, it could perhaps be argued that legal persons (corporations) have also been harmed, principally by government laws and regulations that have aided, inadvertently or otherwise, in the entrenchment of classical management. Conversely, government laws and regulations that have aided in the entrenchment of classical management can be construed as having directly violating the due process clause of the Fifth Amendment, as well as equal protection, in relation to the interests of the public as it pertains to their pursuit of life and liberty.

The information age and digitization of business activities suggest that significant changes are coming to individuals, to business, and to society, if not already present. The management of business (and organizations generally) based on handicraft era (and earlier) preconceptions, practices, and wisdom of a long-ago past seem grossly ill equipped to enable the continued pursuit of life, liberty, and justice (via equal protection). The Constitution gives the federal government authority and responsibility to serve as the nation's steward, to organize and supervise a logical and timely unfolding of laws, regulations, and related actions to assure the survival of the nation and the people's pursuit of life and liberty as times change. Rights retained by the people, otherwise not expressed in the Constitution, are framed by the Ninth Amendment. It is implicit with this context, and that of the Constitution overall, that the federal government is obliged to recognize and ameliorate, in a timely fashion, infringements to life and liberty upon living persons and future generations.

The commerce clause (Article 1, Section 8, clause 3) is used for a variety of purposes, including drug prohibition and civil rights in the context of interstate and intrastate commerce. The Supreme Court has recognized federal government's role in regulating commerce to satisfy the needs for human health and welfare. Therefore, it may be possible to construct additional claims of relief on this basis. In sum, there may be indirect and direct avenues for challenging the constitutionality of classical management itself or the laws and regulations that entrench this now-obsolete method of management.

However, both law and economics have deep connections to the 18th century (Hobbes-Locke era) understanding of Natural Rights, which suggests that constitutional challenges to classical management will bump up against both legal theory and a network of "settled law," thus making it difficult to prosecute grievances. But, perhaps the understanding of Natural Rights needs to be updated for the 21st century and beyond. If such were to happen, it might include the following:

- Freedom beyond free enterprise
- Economic fairness (as distinct from economic equality)
- Human health (more specific forms of "life" and "happiness")
- Social solidarity (in the context of shared human interests)

The concept of Natural Rights should be extended to include the fundamental idea that humans and society must keep up with times and steadily evolve. This can be aided by a welcoming of diverse ideas whose intent is to improve the human condition. Said another way, preconceptions, traditions, and wisdom shroud facts and retard the advancement of knowledge necessary for the maintenance of life, liberty, happiness, and human survival.

Summary

"Every organization constantly deteriorates. And this is especially true of a business organization. It loses customers — through death, through change in location, through the lures of competitors. It loses its personnel from the same causes. Its physical equipment is constantly wearing out and becoming obsolete... It is the primary function of management to rebuild at a rate that exceeds these losses. Management can never rest. If it does, the organization deteriorates. It must attract new customers. It must provide for trained replacement in advance of necessity. It must study new inventions, new devices and better methods. It must initiate a flow of experiments." (Kanuth, 1945)

The dynamic, ever-changing nature of human existence begs for a method of management that is more consonant with reality, facts, and current and future needs. If business (private enterprise) is the central node of reality, applicable to everything, as some imagine, then management is its nucleus. The quality and functionality of the nucleus must be continuously made ever-better to realize more efficient and stable economic growth, and to assure the future health and wealth of a nation. That includes a reduction in the many forms of externalized costs, which for-profit firms have a natural incentive to exploit.

Classical management was constructed in the past to serve the needs of the past, and it is not the sole option going forward. There are other practical resource administration architectures that have been designed to better meet the needs of today and tomorrow. Leaders must be open to better management thinking and better management methods, considering the ever-present need to produce good results. Given the structural deficiencies possessed by classical management, the need for better management is a timely change, reflective of actual needs, not a radical change.

Classical management's connections to the lived traditions of the past carries more force (see Note 16) and makes more sense to people (in part because it embodies a sense of heritage), than progressive management's connections to unlived predictions of possible futures – even for outcomes have been proven to be certain (see Note 17). Any new management method offered must celebrate the past successes of classical management. But it must also connect past failings of classical management's traditions to the interests of two audiences: those who benefited from the traditions and those who were harmed by the traditions. This will assist with the acceptance of the up-front psychological and other costs of change.

This chapter examined four novel approaches to dismantling classical management based on public health policy, duty of care, antitrust, and constitutionality. The dismantling of classical management must usher in the process of robust competition for new, dynamic forms of progressive management practice that is continuously adaptable to better serve the needs of business and humanity now and in the future, while working continuously to make adjustments that minimize expected or known deficiencies. There are many variants of progressive management, each of which has different strengths and weaknesses (see Note 18).

Therefore, there is no one form of progressive management that is suitable for all organizations. Careful evaluation of the choices must precede adoption, and constant monitoring and adjustment must be made following adoption to assure the continued trajectory of progressive management – in spirit, intent, process improvement, and results – and the avoidance of backslide to classical management.

The central idea of this chapter is to better serve the public good by asking leaders to examine available choices and customize solutions to fit the needs of individual organizations and their customers. It is offered in the spirit of strengthening core institutions and expanding social trust, and to impel reasonable examination of viable options that preserve and expand individual freedoms, enhance market competition, and result in a more inclusive, dynamic, and innovative economy. While efficiency is always important, it is now equally important to include resiliency and evolution as core tenets of management thinking and practice, and critical thinking as a manifestation of individual freedom. Another core tenet of management thinking, brought to the forefront by progressive management, is simplification of systems – so easy to say, but hard to do, and therefore requiring management engagement in and support of constant experimentation. This requires leaders to allow employees to think and exercise their creativity daily. The cost of complexity and its paralytic effects on human spirit and initiative must be recognized and acted upon.

It is likely that many, if not most, leaders make their best effort to feign interest in progressive management and their willingness to change. One must ask, are these really the right people to lead us into the future given their continuing commitment to the status quo? Such leaders have had ample opportunities in the past to practice a better management. They need not be given more chances, as time moves mercilessly forward. The social and economic philosophies of the past must be updated and put forever on a path of cumulative improvement. While the market may be a great information processor, it can only partially recognize the needs of humanity. For that, human intelligence must be used. Experts and others must put in the hard work of recognizing and correcting problems and doing so quickly and repeatedly as times change.

Questions to Reflect On

- Why has public health policy not focused on the effects of chronic stress on human physical and mental health? Why has this workplace health risk been ignored?

- What can be done to make corporations less inviting to sociopathic leaders and managers? What structural solutions could be tried? What company-specific solutions could be tried?

- What is the duty of care of executive and non-executive management? Is it defined in corporate codes of conduct or other policies? If not, do these need to be updated? And how will they be enforced?

- The failings of business (antitrust, etc.) have always been assumed to be independent of the management method? Was that a good assumption? By what other means can that bad assumption be corrected?

- What is the role of state and federal government in regulating the conduct of private business in relation to the management method used? Should certain elements of practice, known to be harmful to human health, be disallowed by rule of law?

- What incentives can government offer to assure "good management practice" (akin to "good manufacturing practice" in the pharmaceutical industry; see https://en.wikipedia.org/wiki/Good_manufacturing_practice)?

- How would the flow of information and material be constructed in government "good management practice" guidelines? How would "economies of scale" be addressed in government "good management practice" guidelines?

- What other ways can we get leaders to evolve as time change? How can we help them recognize features of business, leadership, management that are rooted in the past and have no useful function for the present and in the future?

- What other updates need to be made to Natural Rights?

- Dismantling classical management may prove to be easier than imagined. How will that change corporate performance metrics and financial accounting systems?

- Dismantling classical management may prove to be unattainable. What alternatives are there other than the two presented in Chapter 5?

Notes

1. Batch-and-queue is the name given to the common method of processing material and information, wherein a batch of material or information is processed which then sits in queue before moving to the next step in the process, where, again, a batch of material or information is processed which then sits in queue before moving along to the next step in the process, and so on until all steps have been completed to produce the required intermediate or finished product or service. Added together, the sum of queue time is very large compared to the sum of processing time which is small. The accumulation of long queue time in all the needed processes results in long lead-times. Queue time is colloquially referred to as "red tape," and is thought to be merely the result of bureaucratic ineptitude (blaming people). In recent times, the common means for reducing red tape – and thus to theoretically improve productivity, improve and quality, and reduce costs – with the aim of increasing competition and economic efficiency, is to deregulate or privatize businesses or industry. Yet there is another, less well-known way of cutting "red tape" and achieving the same beneficial outcomes, but which is considerably less disruptive and far less expensive – and which reveals the cause to be poor processes (blaming processes) and not bureaucratic ineptitude. It is called flow. Material and information flow are achieved by substantially eliminating queue time via process improvement. Flow is a prominent feature of modern progressive management. The change from classical management to progressive management includes a change from batch-and-queue material and information processing to flow.

2. The classic way business is managed is modeled after how a king or queen ruled their empire. When corporations were first chartered ca. 1600, the method for assembling and coordinating people, material, information, and other resources to achieve vital objectives was taken from the state. Preconceptions of how to manage the empire (in both civil and military affairs) were applied to the task of managing business affairs. Of course, the method for managing business has been modified over the centuries, but it still retains important features characteristic of the method for ruling an empire (*de jure*; by right of ownership; Divine Rights transmuted to Natural Rights, instilling a constant state of fear), and its core aims are nearly identical: to seek gain or advantage over rivals – often by any means possible. The mechanical engineers of the late 1800 and early 1900s sought to advance the practice of management by creating a progressive management method based on cause-and-effect; the scientific method (*de facto*). Thus, they challenged the centuries-old logic of managing business by noble or aristocratic rule. Some business leaders thought fact-based management to be a good idea, though an overwhelming majority did not because it altered their rights and privileges in ways that were distasteful to them. And the aversion to fact-based management continues to this day. At some point in human history, the advancement and survival of humanity, if desired, must be based on facts. That time in human history, the digital age, is upon us. Hence the need to dismantle classical management in business and elsewhere.

3. Characteristically, a results-focus takes on the form of "I don't care how you do it, just get it done." This exposes a great lack of interest in the process and its details by managers. A different view is "good processes yield good results," hence the need to understand processes in detail if one hopes to achieve consistently good results. Sometimes, a good process yields a bad result. This is an indication of an abnormality in the process which must be corrected in order to restore the process to its normal working condition. A results-focus means the cause of the bad result will be ignored in favor of expediency; i.e. managers blaming people for process problems. Needless to say, blaming people for problems does not actually solve any problems and is in obvious contributor to chronic stress, in conflict with "duty of care." Now, imagine a competitor who solves problems instead of blaming people. All other things being equal, the competitor wins.

4. In classical management, new ideas are accepted only if they are sufficiently small or diluted to fit within its interstitial spaces, so as to conserve the established structure and working of classical management. New ideas must fit within established preconceptions and avoid impinging upon the command of expedient conduct; otherwise, they are rejected (see Veblen, 1906). Said another way, the pragmatic knowledge that undergirds the primary aims of business has advanced little over the centuries, as *de jure* (wisdom) stands in authority over *de facto* (science), as shown in Figure 4-3.

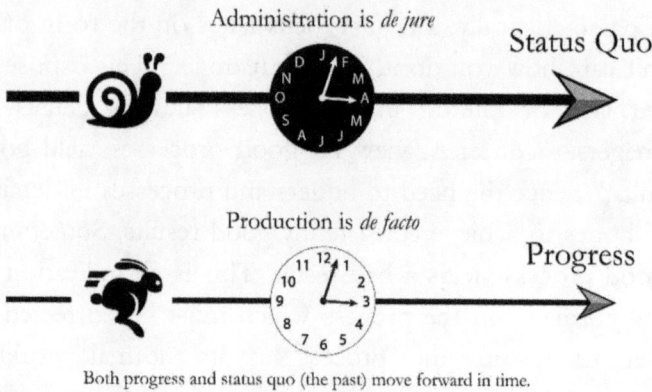

Both progress and status quo (the past) move forward in time.

Figure 4-3. Illustration showing a significant difference between organizational administration based on *de jure* thinking and actions (by right) and productive efforts based on *de facto* thinking and actions (fact-based). Notice the clock faces; the top clock face is demarcated in months, indicative of slow information processing, while the clock face below is demarcated in hours, indicative of faster information processing. Customers exist in the lower clock face, not the upper clock face, and so administration (management) must abandon traditions that produce slow information processing and therefore inhibit the need to keep up with the times. A persistent gap in clock faces generates perceptions of the company being misaligned and mismanaged.

5. If the term "progressive management" bothers you, substitute the words "Modern management" or "Modernized management." The terminology is less important than the need to retire the antiquated management method, classical management. Also, a "method" is a procedure, process, or systematic way of doing something that makes use of a defined corpus of beliefs, mindset, behaviors, skills, and competencies.

6. The prime beneficiaries of classical management – business leaders, politicians, economists, and others in prestige positions – have long been successful at convincing employees, by various means, that this method of management benefits workers. People tend to listen and believe those in authority and are often unaware of the large volume of trustworthy evidence that says otherwise.

7. Adherents to and supporters of classical management, to which neoliberalism is firmly attached (Harvey, 2005), will mount a near-indomitable and sustained defense against its dismantling for fear of losing their grounds of knowledge and their benefits, both real or imagined.

8. In the late 1800s and early 1900s, mechanical engineers found classical management to be incapable in certain technical, human, societal, and financial (wealth-creating) regards (Taylor, 1911; Cooke; 1913; Gilbreth; 1914, Gilbreth, 1914a). They made significant practical modifications to the thinking and practice of classical management, resulting in an early form of progressive management. Its evolution has continued apace since that time (Monden, 1983, Ohno, 1988; Ohno and Mito, 1988) by industrial engineers and others, and to the present day (Figure 4-4).

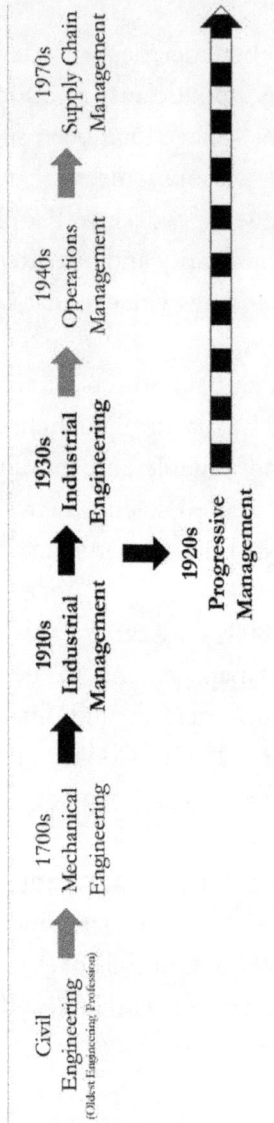

Figure 4-4. Illustration of the emergence (shown in bold) and subsequent evolution (patterned arrow) of progressive management. The diagram could suggest that management education should rightly reside in schools of engineering, given its history, as well as the critical thinking and fact-based approach to engineering education.

9. The longevity of classical management reflects Leaders' preference for the status quo, which is rooted in social, economic, political, philosophical, moral, legal, and historical traditions. Over time, these traditions have been constructed into interlocking systems (institutions) that ensure continuation of the power and privileges associated with leadership. While leaders may recognize the merits of progressive management and may even agree that it is the right thing to do, most are unable to do so because the choice does not actually exist for them. As leaders, they are charged with protecting classical management and the institutions that constructed and support it for the full length of their tenure. Business logic must supersede personal or technical logic. Separating the person (leader) from the institution of leadership and its common requirements and obligations makes it easier to see that acceptance of progressive management it is not a question of executive commitment to change. Leaders' personal desires for substantial improvement in management practice are undercut by obligations to the business and to their peers. Successfully dismantling classical management through public policy, health risk litigation, trade and commerce legislation, and legal challenges to its legitimacy eliminates the need for leaders to voluntarily make a choice. It allows them to save face; they don't have to admit they were wrong, slow to change, and so on.

10. In tending mainly to the financial aspects of business, coupled with grand remuneration through stock options, current-day executives of large corporations function more similarly to that of financial speculators than managers dedicated to the efficient operation of the interconnected

processes that create value for customers (see Veblen, 1901). Management's financial focus and decision-making priorities often have the net effect, intentional or otherwise, of sabotaging employees' ability to do the work. The refrain common heard among workers, "It's amazing we are able to get anything done around here," is uncomfortably close to the truth.

11. Employment under these threatening conditions reflects a severe devaluation of work and human dignity. The single-minded quest for corporate financial efficiency and wealth creation reduces employees' job satisfaction and makes it very difficult to safely and securely traverse life, both at work and at home. Progressive management re-defines work in ways that lessen such threats (Monden, 1982; Byrne, 2012; Hagel et al., 2018). Classical management thoroughly shuns such changes in work definition. Others are finally recognizing the obvious failure of past public policies that made up the "common sense" of ideological traditions, and advocate for new, "good sense" policies based on trustworthy empirical evidence and revitalized (and more accurate) critical thinking (Lindsey et al., 2018). They do, however, continue to ignore how classical management has contributed to the socioeconomic results that they now find undesirable.

12. Other legal doctrines may apply such as strict liability, unconscionability, or *res ipsa loquitur*. One should obviously consult competent and licensed legal counsel for elaboration or other need.

13. Quoting Veblen (1901, p. 191), "The Providential order or of Nature is conceived to work in an effective and just way toward the end to which it tends; and in the economic field this objective end is the material welfare of mankind... The economic laws aimed at and formulated under the guidance of this preconception are laws of what takes place 'naturally' or 'normally, and it is of the essence of things so conceived that in the natural or normal course there is no wasted or misdirected effort." In other words, the foundation of economics is rooted in the divine, and that whatever takes place is, by definition, the most efficient.

Thus, "Whatever is, is right." In the modern (Gilded Age) and post-modern (information age) eras of business practice, technology, and finance, we know the divine preconception is largely invalid. We also know, from analyzing processes using the means and methods of industrial engineering, that waste is ubiquitous, and therefore effort is indeed misdirected. Thus, "Whatever is, is wrong – or at least in need of improvement." This renders classical management obsolete; it is no longer suitable for current and future times. For more on Nature and Natural Rights, see the works of Thomas Hobbes (1588-1679) and John Locke (1632-1704). Think about the difference between "Natural" and actual; the ancient and divine in economics and the latter-day interests and workings of man in economics.

14. Scale and market power are seen by economists as resulting in corporate efficiency. But that is true only of one knows nothing of other management methods or other production systems that do not rely on scale to achieve low

costs or market power to determine prices (see Figure 4-2). Economists understanding of business and economic efficiency is abstract (i.e. input-output models and factors of production). It is not informed by hands-on practice in creating efficient processes, and so their view is necessarily limited and should therefore be far less influential in business and in government economic policy and law.

15. Most CEOs will not voluntarily seek this type of major change, in part because they would be unlikely to receive social confirmation from their peers that their decision was a wise one. In fact, they would more likely be ridiculed by their peers, and therefore seek to avoid unnecessary expose to reputational and career risks. Some CEOs do volunteer to make the switch from classical management to progressive management (Kenney, 2010; Byrne 2012). However, these CEOs typically lead small- to mid-size businesses and have struggled greatly to convince peer CEOs to follow their lead. Logical, fact-based arguments have proven to be largely ineffective. The leaders of large corporations are particularly disinterested in voluntarily replacing classical management with progressive management.

16. The social, economic, political, philosophical, moral, legal, and historical traditions that permeate classical management operate as a kind of comfort food for one's intellectual and emotional pleasure. Connection to the past provides satisfying sentiments and feelings of well-being – which will likely, in time, prove to be illusory.

17. The span of progressive management methods will surely be attacked as "untested theories!" that will "destroy the economy!" and "destroy our way of life!," and similar threadbare distractions, even though none is true. Vested interests will deny both the data and the science, and may claim "culture war!," "redistribution!," and, of course, "socialism!," to preserve their status and benefits. Duty calls when fears are awakened.

18. It has been established through the experience of many that hybrid forms of classical and progressive management do not function well because it is dominated by the residue of classical management. Said another way, even small amounts of classical management can contaminate progressive management and render it largely ineffective (Gryta and Mann, 2018). It is not impossible to wed the two methods, but care must be taken to assure that the combined method evolves in the direction of progressive management.

References

Abelson, R. (2018), "When Hospitals Merge to Save Money, Patients Often Pay More," *The New York Times*, 14 November, https://nyti.ms/2DogCN4

Boston, W. (2018), "Ghosn's U.S. Push Irked Nissan Executives," *The Wall Street Journal*, 18 December, https://www.wsj.com/articles/ghosns-u-s-push-raised-tension-with-nissan-executives-11545129000 (see the slogan, "Grow or go")

Byrne, A. (2012), *The Lean Turnaround: How Business Leaders Use Lean Principles to Create Value and Transform Their Company*, McGraw Hill Education, New York, NY

Buffett, W. (2017), "Warren Buffett on the Importance of Moats," *Nasdaq News*, 28 March https://www.nasdaq.com/article/warren-buffett-on-the-importance-of-moats-cm767018

Cooke, M. (1913), "The Spirit and Social Significance of Scientific Management," *The Journal of Political Economy*, Vol. 21, No. 6, June, pp. 481-493 https://www.jstor.org/stable/pdf/1819267.pdf

Emiliani, B. (2015), *Speed Leadership: A New Way to Lead for Rapidly Changing Times*, The CLBM, LLC, Wethersfield, Conn.

Gilbreth, F. (1914), *Primer of Scientific Management*, Van Nostrand Co., New York, NY

Gilbreth, L. (1914a), *The Psychology of Management*, Sturgis and Walton Co., New York, NY

Goh, J., Pfeffer, J., and Stefanos, Z., (2016), "The Relationship Between Workplace Stressors and Mortality and Health Costs in the United States," *Management Science*, Vol. 62, Issue 2, pp. 608-628

Gryta, T. and Mann, T. (2018), "GE Powered the American Century—Then It Burned Out," *The Wall Street Journal*, 14 December, https://www.wsj.com/articles/ge-powered-the-american-centurythen-it-burned-out-11544796010

Hagel J., Brown, J., and Wooll, M. (2018), "Redefine work: The Untapped Opportunity for Expanding Value," *Deloitte Insight*, December, https://www2.deloitte.com/content/dam/insights/us/artic les/4779_Redefine-work/DI_Redefine-work.pdf

Harvey, D. (2005), *A Brief History of Neoliberalism*, Oxford University Press, London, U.K.

Heminway, J. (2008), *Stress: Portrait of a Killer*, National Geographic Special Documentary Video, 24 September, https://www.imdb.com/title/tt1278078/

Jefferson, T., et al. (1788), "The Constitution of the United States," *The National Archives*, https://www.archives.gov/founding-docs/constitution

Kendall, B. (2018), "StarKist to Plead Guilty to Price-Fixing Canned Tuna," *The Wall Street Journal*, 18 October, https://www.wsj.com/articles/starkist-to-plead-guilty-to-price-fixing-canned-tuna-1539898195

Kenney, C. (2010), *Transforming Health Care: Virginia Mason Medical Center's Pursuit of the Perfect Patient Experience*, CRC Press, Boca Raton, Florida

Khan, L. (2017), "Amazon's Antitrust Paradox," *The Yale Law Journal*, Vol. 126, No. 3, pp. 710-805, January, https://www.yalelawjournal.org/note/amazons-antitrust-paradox

Khan, L. (2018), "The Ideological Roots of America's Market Power Problem,"
The Yale Law Journal, Vol. 127, pp. 960-979, 4 June, https://www.yalelawjournal.org/forum/the-ideological-roots-of-americas-market-power-problem

Knauth, O. (1945), "The Dilemma of Management," *Advanced Management Quarterly Journal*, Volume X, No. 1, January-March

Landhuis, E. (2018), "How Dad's Stresses Get Passed Along to Offspring," *Scientific American*, Volume 319, Issue 5, November
https://www.scientificamerican.com/article/how-dads-stresses-get-passed-along-to-offspring/

Lindsey, B., Wilkinson, W., Teles, S, and Hammond, S. (2018), "The Center Can Hold: Public Policy for an Age of Extremes," Niskanen Center Policy Essay, 18 December https://niskanencenter.org/wp-content/uploads/2018/12/Niskanen-vision-paper-final-PDF.pdf

Mathews, A. (2018), "Hospital Chain Settles U.S. Suit Over Stifled Competition," *The Wall Street Journal*, 15 November, https://www.wsj.com/articles/hospital-chain-settles-u-s-suit-over-stifled-competition-1542316218

Maxcy, G. and Silberston, A. (1959), *The Motor Industry*, George Allen & Unwin Ltd., London, U.K., p. 94, Figure 2

Monden, Y. (1983), *Toyota Production System: Practical Approach to Production Management*, Engineering and Management Press, Norcross, Georgia

Ohno, T. (1988), *Toyota Production System – Beyond Large-Scale Production*, Productivity Press, Portland, OR

Ohno, T. and Mito, S. (1988), *Just-In-Time For Today and Tomorrow*, Productivity Press, Cambridge, Mass.

Pfeffer, J. (2018), *Dying for a Paycheck: How Modern Management Harms Employee Health and Company Performance - And What We Can Do About It*, HarperBusiness, New York, NY

Rowland, C. (2018), "Investigation of Generic 'Cartel' Expands to 300 Drugs," *The Washington Post*, 9 December, https://wapo.st/2rrKD7F?tid=ss_tw&utm_term=.46375b1 c67ee

Sapolsky, R. (2018), "How Economic Inequality Inflicts Real Biological Harm," *Scientific American*, Volume 319, Issue 5, November, https://www.scientificamerican.com/article/how-economic-inequality-inflicts-real-biological-harm/

Stone, D. (1989), "Causal Stories and the Formation of Policy Agendas," *Political Science Quarterly*, Vol. 104, No. 2, pp. 281-300

Taylor, F. W. (1911), *The Principles of Scientific Management*, Harper and Brothers, New York, NY

Thiel, P. (2014), "Competition Is for Losers: If you want to create and capture lasting value, look to build a monopoly," *The Wall Street Journal*, 12 September, https://www.wsj.com/articles/peter-thiel-competition-is-for-losers-1410535536

Veblen, T. (1901), "Industrial and Pecuniary Employments," *Publications of the American Economic Association*, Volume 2. No. 1, February, pp. 190-235

Veblen, T. (1904), *The Theory of Business Enterprise*, Charles Scribner's Sons, New York, NY

Veblen, T. (1906), "The Place of Science in Modern Civilization," *The American Journal of Sociology*, Volume 11, No. 5, March

Veblen, T. (1921), *The Engineers and the Price System*, B.W. Huebsch, Inc., New York, NY

Wu, T. (2018), *The Curse of Bigness: Antitrust in the New Gilded Age*, Columbia Global Reports, Columbia University, New York, NY

5

Two Alternatives To Lean Management

Why Do We Need Alternatives?

Chapters 1, 2, and 3 show that business leaders have little interest in improving the practice of management, while Chapter 4 offers ways to force them to reconsider their aversion and accept progressive management. Leaders will commit the organizations to small improvements, and they may occasionally make small improvements to their own management practice, but they are unwilling to do away with classical management and replace it with progressive forms of management such as Lean. Protecting vested rights and vested interests is the most important thing. Let's assume that executives are immovable on this point. What then, given that management still needs improvement?

Though Lean management is a simpler derivative version of Toyota's management system, it remains complex and difficult for the vast majority of executives to understand and practice, so they invariably delegate it to lower levels. The evidence for this is clear. In all the visits that I have made to companies over the years, the same picture emerges: pervasive use of various Lean tools (value stream maps, A3 reports, etc.) without an understanding of the underlying objectives or way of thinking. While there are some exceptions, this is the typical case, evident in 1998 as it is in 2018. Clearly, Lean has struggled to establish itself in corporations beyond the decorative use of some tools, despite its many worthy and fascinating features.

The reality is that Lean is not relevant to business leader's interests – at least not after 30 years, and perhaps never. This suggests that Lean management promoters must challenge their own preconceptions: Do business leaders want "transformation?" Do they want a new system of management? The evidence indicates that they do not, and efforts to re-package Lean management to make it more acceptable to leaders is unlikely to succeed. And Toyota, admirable as their management method may be, is largely irrelevant. Most executives consider Toyota's management to be unique to Toyota and its particular interests.

Lean management has failed to offer business owners and corporate executives the things that they want and need most: the economic, social, political, historical, philosophical, and business distinctions that certify power, prestige, and dozens of other important things they desire. Despite this reality, Lean continues along the same path established decades ago. Given these circumstances, what, then, are some alternatives?

Alternative One – iMaP

Generally, people like new things if they can easily see its benefits and if its costs (money and other forms of cost) are reasonable. Lean management has long been seen by most business owners and corporate executives as lacking benefits and unreasonably high in costs. So, Lean must be reimagined if the practice of management is to move forward. An improved management practice – call it "iMaP" – must offer expanded benefits and much lower costs to business owners and corporate executives. How would one get business owners and executives to accept an improved management practice, while also recognizing they need not sacrifice the power, prestige, and dozens of other important things they desire?

First, begin by introducing iMaP differently than the way Lean was introduced and the way in which Lean has been elaborated upon over time, both of which caused immense misunderstandings and confusion. Obviously, iMaP must be simple and easy to understand – and not just for business owners and executives, but for employees, suppliers, investors, customers, bankers, investment analysts, politicians, and so on.

iMaP operates on three principles: 1) "Go with the flow" regarding the wants and needs of business owners and corporate executives, 2) Material and information flow generates the lowest total costs, and 3) Those who benefit the most from higher enterprise value created by flow (executives and shareholders) must bear the cost in the form of above-average compensation for non-executive employees. The framework for iMaP is as follows:

- Daily cost reduction conducted in ways that do not harm employees or other stakeholders, to assure speed and responsiveness to changing business conditions
- Productivity improvement to assist business growth, featuring re-deployment of labor to intensify innovation and to control and stabilize employment
- Flow is the standard method for company-wide cost reduction, to control demand-driven outputs (quantity) and assure quality in every process in the company

The means for achieving flow is the designated responsibility of labor, technical staff, supervision, managers, and general managers. Together, they use their own creativity and innovations to discover and learn the many ways to make material and information flow without interruption. Senior leaders – vice presidents, president, CEO, and boards of directors – maintain their responsibilities as usual, but must adhere to two rules:

- Do not disrupt flow or efforts to create material and information flow
- Above-average compensation for employees (paycheck, especially)

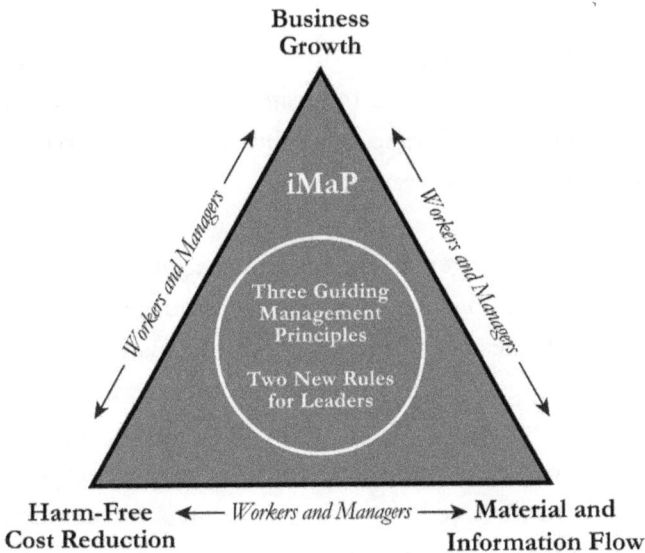

Figure 5-1. Schematic representation of the iMaP concept.

iMaP strips out all the complexity associated with Lean management. It strips out all the uniqueness and complexity associated with Toyota's management system as well. It strips out the problems and unhealthy nonsense that is generated by transformation, cliques, cults, and movements, etc. But, importantly, iMaP retains the core thinking and objectives behind TPS.

iMaP places just two rules on senior management. Complying with the rules will motivate non-executive employees to make the changes necessary to achieve or improve flow. They will develop their own methods and create their own language and tools in pursuit of the objective, flow. Importantly, the need for training senior leaders is greatly reduced and centers upon comparing and contrasting continuous flow vs. blocked flow. A strong conceptual understanding of flow may be all that is required. There is no need to create "Lean leaders," or other specialized type of executive, few of which have been created in the last 30 years anyway.

The middle manager no longer has the most difficult job. That now belongs to the general manager who must negotiate the results of material and information flow with senior managers. For example, conflicts arising from incorrect metrics, unit vs. total cost focus, etc. iMaP respects people. In particular, non-executive employees, by giving them the freedom to do great things for themselves, the company, and its stakeholders. Simultaneously, it respects and satisfies the power, prestige, and dozens of other important things that business owners and corporate executives desire.

While iMaP may not be the ideal that some people want, it is the more practical solution that many could have.

Alternative Two – Speed Leadership

A second alternative is to reimagine leadership, in the hope that it has a spillover effect in improving management practice. But, what, if anything, do business leaders want in terms of leadership development? It seems that what business leaders want must fit the following criteria:

1. Low cost
2. Simple to understand and practice
3. Easy to deploy across the organization
4. Deliverable by internal trainers
5. Long-lasting
6. Evolves in step with actual needs
7. Independent of management system
8. Independent of work area (office, shop, field)
9. Independent of function (finance, HR, IT, etc.)
10. Hands-on active learning
11. Participants create something useful
12. Connects learning to actual experiences
13. Customizable to meet individual needs
14. Engaging, rigorous, analytical, and memorable
15. Fast and effective translation into practice
16. Expand the internal pool of leaders

They want something that **helps leaders do what they do better**, within the frameworks of the long-existing philosophy of business and the classical management method. They do not want to replace what they know and do very well with something that is complex and which takes a long time to learn.

Recognizing this, I set out to create something new that met all 16 criteria. What I developed was based on the thinking associated with Toyota's management system that I had learned over many years (kaizen, in particular), but without the complexity or need for "transformation" or the replacement of classical management. I found something that could fit within any existing management system and philosophy of business, and therefore be acceptable to leaders, and which could result in improvement that would benefit employees, business, and society. I named it "Speed Leadership."

Starting around 2011, I started to reimagine leadership in terms of processes rather than as an unpredictable jumble of daily activities. I identified 15 leadership processes that occupy most of a leader's time day-to-day. That led to the easy identification of errors that leaders make in each leadership process. The errors can then be corrected using various simple methods that have long been in use by most corporations. What makes Speed Leadership work is the fact that the existence of the errors, some 20 to 40 errors per leadership process, are undeniable. Even top leaders will admit the errors exist and that they are pervasive throughout the organization.

The leadership processes and errors are simple to comprehend, and the methods for eliminating the errors are simple as well. Why should leaders want to eliminate the errors that they make in their leadership processes? It is because the errors negatively impact followers; it results in the inability of employees to get their work done. Time is a precious resource, and leadership process errors also negatively impacts time; it takes more time for employees to complete their tasks, which increases costs. Completing tasks in more time than is necessary, along with higher costs, diminishes competitiveness and profitability.

In addition, leadership process errors have a negative impact on information and information flow. Leadership process errors reduce the quality of information received by executives. It also reduces the flow of information to executives. The loss of information fidelity and the reduced flow of information combine to produce time delays, errors in decision-making, higher costs, and reduced competitiveness. It also diminishes teamwork and management's credibility.

The connections between leadership process errors and time, information, and information flow is a simple cause-and-effect relationship that anyone can easily understand. No executive wants to make errors or bad decisions. The fact that both are routine occurrences is the result of a few blind spots. Executives who can commit to making some small changes to their leadership processes will become better and more effective leaders – without the need for wholesale transformation of their beliefs, behaviors, and competencies as is demanded by both Lean and TMS. All that is needed is a willingness to acknowledge the existence of the errors and a desire to make some reasonable adjustments. Speed Leadership is easy to learn, practical, and doable.

In 2015, I wrote a small, 150-page book titled: *Speed Leadership: A New Way to Lead for Rapidly Changing Times* (second edition). The book summarizes these ideas and presents work that was tested for years in my graduate leadership course and later in short corporate training courses. The book outlines the basic ideas and presents several simple ideas for daily improvement. However, Speed Leadership has evolved considerably since 2015, so what you read in the book does not include the many advances (simplifications) that have been made since then in the understanding and practice of Speed Leadership.

Please read the book and let me know if you think Speed Leadership is right for your organization. Unlike Lean, where "everything must change," Speed Leadership offers something vastly reduced in scale and scope, yet is simple and effective, and which can still have a very large positive impact throughout an organization.

If you are a long-time Lean practitioner and frustrated or losing interest in Lean, Speed Leadership provides an opportunity for you to retain your commitment to improvement but also move on and engage a new subject of interest. You can leverage your knowledge of Lean and apply it in new ways. There is no shame in doing that.

Final Thoughts

The Triumph of Classical Management

It is clear that classical management has triumphed over progressive management, beginning with Scientific Management, to Toyota's management system, and on to its derivative, Lean management. The winning ways of classical management, made possible by executive's strict adherence to traditions, have prevailed, and may prevail well in the future. In the meantime, those who are committed to Lean management, or whatever succeeds it, will valiantly press onward. They will find some success here and there, but overall, they will continue to encounter executive's archaic preconceptions about business, economics, politics, and so on. The preconceptions that disable progress are ever-present, if not in the current leadership team, then surely in the one that follows or the one after that. Classical management may go in abeyance for some amount of time, but not for all time. Any displacement of classical management in organizations is likely to be only temporary.

It is possible that conditions could change, perhaps due to political pressure, a global crisis of some sort, or other calamity, such that most of the archaic preconceptions that prevent Lean transformation and the evolution of management practice will start to dissolve away. If that happens, the precious "beginner's mind" will emerge among senior executives. The archaic preconceptions that concatenate from transmitters to receivers over generations of executives will be disrupted. Interesting new opportunities will be generated that benefit both business and society.

Yet, the dissolution of archaic preconceptions alone does not signal victory; there are other problems to contend with. Progressive management is difficult for anyone, especially senior executives, to understand and practice. Even though this book solves certain problems, future results may not be so different compared to today's results. After all, few business leaders are intrinsically motivated to make the long-term commitment needed to learn Lean, much like the long-term commitment that is needed to learn how to play a musical instrument well.

In the past, problems such as Lean transformation failures, have been largely ignored by Lean promoters in favor of highlighting success stories. Those who promote progressive management in the future cannot repeat this mistake yet again (it afflicted Scientific Management as well). There is as much to learn from failure as from success, and likely more. There must be contemporaneous recognition and acceptance of the existence failure, immediate engagement of diverse resources focused on problem-solving, and rapid dissemination of results to the public.

Lean advocates must also face the facts. They have preconceptions about leaders, change, and improvement that stand in the way of understanding what executives want. It does not make sense to push a product onto executives that they do not want – especially when it is not competitive against the long-established methods used by executives to create wealth or achieve customer satisfaction. Lean can seem akin to a product that has been overdesigned and which therefore is too complex, confuses the user, too expensive, and too time-consuming to learn. Will decontenting Lean help improve the product? Will better marketing help? Probably not, as many have tied to do both and achieved little or nothing. Sometimes the inferior product, classical management, is better at satisfying the users' needs. That some may be harmed by zero-sum classical management practice, such as employees, suppliers, or communities, is immaterial given the acceptance among executives for the "there must be winners and losers" preconception. Interesting things could happen if this preconception were to go away.

This is but one preconception among a large set of preconceptions repetitively transmitted and received by the inhabitants of the upper-echelon in both business and society, where the societal component is made up of those in close proximity to the institution of business such as lawyers, professors, and journalists. In other words, preconceptions favorable to the perpetuation of vested rights and vested interests are reinforced through social information sharing – face-to-face or via mediated sources such as education, training, newspapers, magazines, the Internet, etc. Together, these generate the executive culture that resists Lean management and turns acceptance of Lean into a major political problem.

This results in a shared philosophy of business that is self-contained in its professed coherence and reduction to daily practice among executives (but which is unable to withstand rigorous logical criticism; therefore, pseudologic), thus creating metaphysical leaders from former inhabitants of the material world. The classical management philosophy of business has its origins in Western thought, dating from Roman times through 18th and 19th century French and English moral philosophy and political economy scholars. The associated sentiments and preconceptions are rarely tested, resulting in a theoretical or idealized understanding of business and work processes that, while intelligible to executives, is far from the truth.

Lean management, based on Toyota's production system, embodies an Eastern philosophy of business built on a different set of sentiments and preconceptions (and able to withstand rigorous logical criticism) – a few of which are the same as Western preconceptions, but altered to conform to a social capitalism (vs. market capitalism) understanding of business and economics. Importantly, preconceptions are periodically tested to determine if they remain useful in the ever-changing world of human experience. It is an enormous challenge to fully understand the Toyota way of thinking. Lean is not as difficult to understand, but it too remains challenging because of the basic shift in perspective from zero-sum to non-zero-sum outcomes. However, executives can gain a good-enough understanding relatively quickly if they are open-minded, and they will be delighted at how much progress can be made in just a few short years.

An open mind, willing to test one's preconceptions, is fundamental to innovation and advancement. Managers encourage employees to be innovative in their work processes or in the creation of new products and services because it usually results in favorable business outcomes. Yet, managers do not apply this thinking to their own work.

If the function of management is seen as a service to business stakeholders, then it is subject to innovation and advancement in practice. If, on the other hand, the function of management is seen as an instrument for protecting vested rights and vested interests, then it necessarily requires a closed mind and blind acceptance of the entire set of archaic preconceptions and associated sentiments and traditions. Serving one's self is honorable, while serving others is not.

More than one hundred years of empirical evidence informs us that executives view protecting vested rights and vested interests as far more important than innovation and advancement in leadership and management practice. While one can apprehend or perhaps even sympathize with that perspective, it is nevertheless unfortunate because, while classical management is great for executives, it is lousy for everyone else. Business underperforms, society suffers, and humans cannot realize their full potential.

- Fin -

Appendix

Selected Readings

The essays contained in the following pages were selected from blog posts written in 2018. They are relevant to the topic at hand and make important points not yet addressed. But, as discrete ideas written in a more informal style, they are better suited for this section of the book. The short essays are titled:

Business Philosophy Triangle

Redistribution and Deservingness

The Business Case for Ignoring Lean

Lean is an Intangible Asset

Problem-Solving and Human Progress

In addition, I have included images that offer visual explanations of phenomena described in this book, under the heading:

Six Pictures Tell All

Business Philosophy Triangle

Chapters 1, 2, and 3 answered research questions from economic, social, political, and historical perspectives, while Chapter 4 addressed legal perspectives. In addition to these perspectives, business affairs are conducted by leaders with a general philosophy in mind, informed by Western philosophy, which is the ground upon which economic thought generally rests. The basis for executive resistance and disinterest in Lean management must therefore also be rooted in their philosophy of business.

Most business leaders are raised in the tradition of Western business thinking and practices, as informed by economic liberalism, hierarchical management control, and conventional leadership routines. Leaders raised in these traditions clearly have great difficulty understanding the Eastern philosophy and traditions associated with Toyota's management practice and its derivative, Lean. So, this perspective is also worth examining, for it will yield additional insights and understanding of how to overcome executive resistance and disinterest in Lean management.

The philosophy of business is framed by three distinct Western philosophical "isms:" Realism, Idealism, and Pragmatism (Lodge, 1945). In the context of leading a business (i.e. the high-level view), philosophical realism would be a view associated with challenging or difficult business conditions, such as severe competition or economic recession. Philosophical idealism is associated with difficult but improving business conditions, such as economic recovery. Philosophical pragmatism is associated with sales and profit growth, as is typically the case in economic expansions. Thus, the guiding philosophy adopted by business leaders varies with business conditions (i.e. the business cycle).

All employees broadly conduct their work in ways guided by each one of the three "isms." Executives and finance people, driven by realism, examine the business based on facts as represented by data such as in spreadsheets or dashboards, objectivity from their high position in the hierarchy, and need for uniformity, and conformity. Employees such as designers and mechanical engineers, driven by idealism, rely on insight, mind, spirit, dreams, and subjectivity to create new products and services. Employees such as industrial engineers, manufacturing engineers, and Lean people, driven by pragmatism, are action-oriented, and favor learn-by-doing, experimentation, and trial-and-error.

Post-1980, business has shifted towards realism (economic rationalism). Realism is favored by executives of large companies, and it is the root business philosophy for sellers' markets (oligopoly, monopoly) which are highly prized by business leaders. When corporate existence or profits are threatened, executives become strong realists. Generally, realism favors de-socializing, de-humanizing, and de-experimentation, and realism tightly couples with the pseudologic of executive instinct and sentiments. Too much realism (economic rationalism) eventually leads to financial problems, while financial problems lead to increased realism, not increased pragmatism, which is how companies enter into downward spirals.

Idealists are the creators; skilled artisans and craftsmen, independent and prideful, and are held in high regard by management and therefore often sheltered from turbulent business conditions (such as layoffs). They enjoy higher social standing than pragmatists. Pragmatists are creative, inventive, and innovative, yet they possess strong "just do it," "do it now," "try it and see," progressive attitudes. Their pragmatism takes two forms: social (teamwork) and experimental (scientific method and its derivatives). Promotion from skilled worker (pragmatist) to manager (realist) is a difficult philosophical transition to make, which explains why many are unhappy in their management job or seen by subordinates as poor managers. Idealism and realism are "office" philosophies, Pragmatism is the "factory" (or "producer") philosophy.

Pragmatism is the root business philosophy for businesses facing competitive buyers' markets. Lacking market power, leaders of startups must be pragmatic, because they seek to scrap the past and create a better tomorrow. That requires then to lead efforts to experiment rapidly.

Given this philosophical blueprint, it is apparent that pragmatic Lean management does not appeal to executives' imaginations. Nor does it appeal to workers' imaginations because they fear realist executives will drive them harder (see Chapter 2, Figure 2-1a). As might be expected, executives who cannot empathize with idealists and pragmatists generate conflicts, which reduces innovation and productivity. It also creates uncertainly among employees as the leaders' philosophy of business varies according macroeconomic conditions and market power. Executives drift from one philosophy to another based on need or circumstance, causing executives to appear inconsistent or hypocritical, thus sacrificing influence among stakeholders. When the three philosophies clash among executives, realists win, idealists stay, and pragmatists leave or are dismissed. Lean management will not take root in businesses dominated by executives with strong realist philosophy, though they may accede to it (or, more likely, parts of it) in times of crisis – but return to classical management as business conditions improve.

This provides a useful philosophical explanation for executive resistance to and disinterest in Lean management, one that also offers a potential solution.

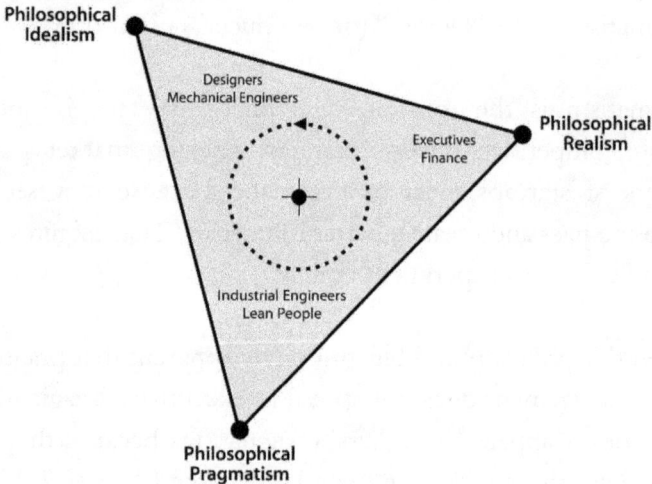

Figure A-1. The business philosophy triangle (BPT).

First, let's assume that the employees identified in each corner of the business philosophy triangle (and others like them) have developed habit (by education, job, and experience) of residing in their respective corners. Now take the case of CEOs, who will reside almost exclusively in the upper right corner (philosophical realism). Employees stuck in their corners will be bad for the business and its customers, because they will have difficulty responding to changes that are imposed on them by competition and business cycles. Their response will be both slow and off-target (e.g. the inverse of what is actually required).

Furthermore, it should be obvious that CEOs mismanage when, through their leadership, they get the company (managers and workers) stuck in one corner or another. This points to a potential solution: CEOs and their direct reports must frequently circulate among the philosophies – the dotted circle – to assure that they do not get stuck in their own favorite philosophical corner. That means they must understand the work processes of other people and empathize with them. CEOs are responsible for all three philosophies that exist in business, not just their own favored realist philosophy. Executives must possess all three philosophies – at least in rough balance, if not weighted towards pragmatism, to avoid the business problems that are invariably generated by excessive realism and idealism.

The BPT suggests that leaders, typically absent from the workplace, must be taught the need for circulating around the triangle – i.e., dotted circle, which represents the workplace. They must be taught how to circulate around the triangle effectively. And they must be taught the atypical business conditions under which it may be wise to retreat to one corner – but only for the duration it is needed – then return to a balanced position soon after business conditions stabilize. The BPT also suggests numerous practical process that executives can practice to avoid the problem of executive resistance to progressive management. Kaizen is a useful method for identifying and implementing solutions to this common social problem of separation between workers and managers, and absentee leadership.

Finally, look carefully at the business philosophy triangle and ask these questions:

- Are our company's problems caused by executives being stuck in philosophical corner of the triangle (thus, absentee leaders)? Do we experience the same recurring problems because of that?
- How do we restore philosophical balance in the executive team? How do we develop future leaders to be both philosophically balanced and present?
- What does the BPT mean in relation to the responsibilities of human resource executives and Boards of Directors?
- What does the BPT mean for employees and investors? Communities and suppliers?

Reference

Lodge, R. (1945), *Philosophy of Business*, University of Chicago Press, Chicago, Illinois

Redistribution and Deservingness

In addition to the economic, social, political, historical, and legal factors cited for failing to transition to progressive management, there is another factor; an important business reason – one that executives raised in classical management have an aversion to addressing: Redistribution.

The full embrace of progressive management sets in motion a giant redistribution problem; a redistribution of pretty much everything, to greater or lesser extents, that exists in a business. Lean transformation means a redistribution of wealth, power, control, prestige, status, time, knowledge, responsibilities, human interaction, recognition, training, focus, priorities, work, energy, beliefs (sentiments), behaviors (for leaders and non-leaders), competencies, rewards, historical preferences, prejudices, support, and perquisites, to name just a few.

It is no secret that most business leaders view wage earners and professional staff negatively from a social status perspective, and for executives to view themselves as higher status and more worthy, or of greater value to the organization, than others. In addition, there is the question of whether wage earners and professional staff deserve the benefits that come from redistribution. If the perception among executives is that wage earners and professional staff are well-compensated yet still underperform to business needs or executives' expectations (real or perceived), then progressive management in its full form will not be forthcoming. In other words, wage earners and professional staff do not deserve progressive management.

Wage earners and professional staff have legitimate needs with respect to doing their job, which progressive management can actualize, to help the business grow and become more successful. But those needs will go unfulfilled so long as the budget owners view "them," the primary beneficiaries of redistribution, as inferior. Therefore, undeservingness fully justifies zero-sum economic, social, and political outcomes.

So even though the continuation of classical management does broad harm to the many – humanity, the economy, the environment, and so on – executives continue to practice it because it serves their interest to avoid redistribution. This explains why efforts to "sell" progressive management to business leaders are destined to fail. The logic of business (money-making) and the logic of progressive management are not aligned.

Toyota's management system, and its derivative Lean management, set off a revolution in consciousness about what leadership and management should be. But it also generated a backlash because Lean management is not commensurate with business leaders' view of the workforce and its view of entitlement – a right to individual respect, challenging work, social fulfillment, and economic prosperity – and its achievement via the wholesale redistribution of business affairs.

It is difficult to imagine Lean making further inroads into the practice of management if such fundamental problems as this continue to be ignored by Lean's promoters and advocates.

What is easy to imagine is Lean promoters and advocates continuing to complain about how business leaders don't "get it," continued glorification of the few business leaders that do "get it," and perpetually wishing for more leaders like them. It is also easy to image them continuing to proffer models (e.g. Lean transformation "houses") whose most basic demands infringe upon leaders' vested rights and interests. That is not a practical route to success.

The Business Case for Ignoring Lean

The business case used by business leaders to ignore Lean is deceptively simple: Synchronizing supply with demand is bad business practice. It is undesirable because it deleverages free market price determination, which undermines profits.

In most of the world, companies operate in a free market, which means it is a competitive market governed by the laws of supply and demand. This is a means of determining prices – a "price-system" – based on the quantity supplied by producers and the quantity demanded by users. Rarely are the two in equilibrium, and for good a reason: Profits. In particular, the gain in profit depending on the price that the market will bear as determined by supply and demand at any given point in time. (Note that "supply and demand" applies to the company itself, as well as the goods and services a company produces).

There are certain facts of business thinking and practice that are relevant to the business case for ignoring Lean: Owners and managers very much want to avoid gluts (buyers' markets), and so they are always seeking to achieve sellers' markets and therefore gain pricing power – in other words, an overwhelming fear of competition. Business leaders are generally distrustful, and specifically distrustful of stakeholders such as suppliers, employees, and competitors – and often their peers as well. They do not like workers because they can neither be capitalized nor depreciated.

Efficiency, productivity, and cost reduction are of interest, but these are best achieved by procuring new machine technologies (machine-based process improvement); there is far less interest in human-based technologies (the brain; ideas and creativity) in large part because technology decides who wins and who loses. Business leaders love economies of scale, more for scale than for economies (though, EoS does amortize waste, which is so much easier to do than eliminate waste). They are self-interested and seek to maximize their own gains, with salesmanship, marketing campaigns, and sales promotions featuring prominently in efforts to maximize gains. They have a zero-sum mindset, where one party's loss is another party's gain, and so they always seek to win at someone else's expense.

Winning is paramount for leaders, even if only in appearance, because it confers status, authority, and the right to maintain the status quo – which is why, for example, challenging leaders to adopt Lean management or practice Lean methods and tools, usually fails. They believe a business must "grow or die," which is actually a statement about the importance of gaining leverage over other stakeholders, to win. They love deal-making and are always on the hunt for mergers and acquisitions. The "synergies" (cost savings) that help sell the deal rarely materialize because they are not important. The bigger the company (scale), the more it is able to "buy cheap and sell dear;" to gain market power in order to exert leverage over suppliers to obtain low prices and leverage over customers to obtain high prices, and generally to gain tangible and intangible concessions from any party that the company interacts with.

Business is the pursuit of profit (gain) "with the frame of mind that is native to the countinghouse." Managers are required to produce a profit, free income, which is embedded in price as well as determined by price. Therefore, there is an incentive to withhold supply to achieve a sellers' market and gain pricing power. But, as demand varies over time, supply must be throttled to avoid overproduction and the creation of a buyers' market. The ability to throttle output is of supreme importance and is aided by economies of scale (and sales incentives), which greatly extends the range of available throttling positions and price points. In other words, the cost savings achievable with economies of scale is of less importance than the number of price points and price increases that are achievable.

The image below shows the view of price, cost, and profit for classical management and for Toyota management. For classical management, cost is understood to be comprised of fixed and variable elements. For Toyota, cost is the sum of value-added plus waste plus unevenness plus unreasonableness. For both, profit as the sum of retained earnings plus cash distributed to shareholders plus taxes.

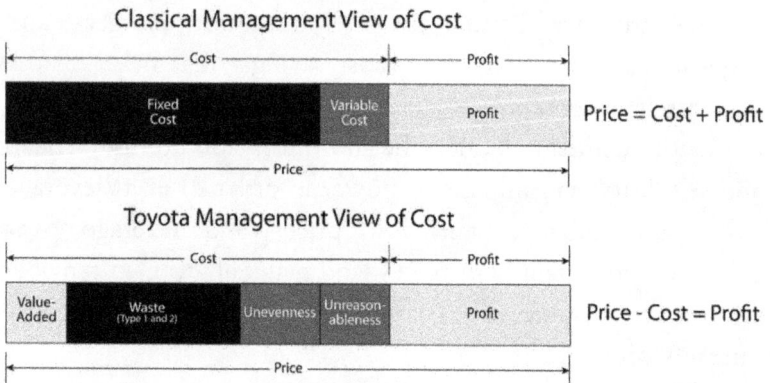

Figure A-2. Money view of cost (classical management) versus process view of cost (progressive management).

The money view of cost problems is a frame that leads to a narrow choice of possible solutions. In contrast, the process view of cost problems is a frame that leads to a wide range of possible solutions. The classical management view of cost shows a major defect in the understanding of costs (fixed cost/variable cost) that spans economics, finance, investment banking, private equity, accounting, and, of course, management decision-making, and which, in turn, has far-reaching consequences. Namely, it sabotages Lean, and is one of the many controlling mechanisms used by leaders to reject Lean, knowingly or otherwise. In economics, accounting, etc., costs exist abstractly outside the reality of physical processes as fixed costs and variable costs, and so management's response to cost problems is different *(de jure)* than the response to cost problems understood in physical reality *(de facto)*.

The Toyota management view of cost shows how the defect was repaired: via the realization that processes generate costs. If you improve the process – with an understanding of value-added work, waste, unevenness, and unreasonableness – then the cost is reduced (inclusive of improvement in all the non-financial parameters cited above). The result, if process improvement is practiced consistently, is the development of human capabilities, improved management decision-making, and production of consistent business results.

CEOs and CFOs think in terms of abstract fixed costs and variable costs (and spreadsheets, also abstract, as is money itself) while workers think in terms of physical processes. Leaders cannot understand costs if they do not understand physical processes, and so the quality of their decision-making will be greatly reduced and always cluster around the same set of solutions that every other CEO and CFO uses. There is no creativity or originality in problem-solving when cost problems in business exist as abstractions. And that is why business always moves confidently in the direction of that which has been previously established. In other words, status quo.

Executives' unwillingness to learn the physical reality of processes and costs is a conscious withdrawal of discovery, learning, and enlightenment. It is purposeful underemployment of executive capability, in preference for whim, and which in turn assures worker capability is likewise underemployed. In making this fateful decision, executives assure that the business will run with waste, unevenness, and unreasonableness as features of management practice rather than as flaws in management practice. This is an integral part of the design of classical management in market economies. Therefore, the process view of cost is unwelcome, which means Lean is unwelcome.

Rejecting process, and therefore rejection of sequential or consecutive change and cause-and-effect, means that business remains on a largely non-scientific and non-evolutionary footing. When change does occur, it is but a small difference from the previous way of thinking and doing things; often a difference largely in name only. Management decision-making favors as hoc, whatever-is-right-for-the-moment decisions, and thus fails to build on the success and failures of self or others – as is the case in science or engineering, which are clearly evolutionary. The same mistakes are repeated again and again because management ignores process and causation. This part of the business case for ignoring Lean fits neatly into the overall business case of not wanting to synchronize supply with demand, because doing so means having to pay close attention to processes – all processes in a business, not just production processes. It places an unreasonable demand on leaders to know how to improve processes, which would significantly transform their view of costs (as well as profit and prices).

When a company's objective is to make money (classical management), management's focus is on prices. Specifically, increasing unit prices to gain more free income (profit; i.e. wealth). Waste, unevenness, and unreasonableness raise both market prices and profit (as a percent of cost) — with prices having been set by managers. Greater mismatches in supply and demand, especially those which favor the producer (and which generate greater amounts of waste, unevenness, and unreasonableness), result in higher prices for customers. Working to obtain a sellers' market – by mergers and acquisitions, patents, economies of scale, monopoly, or other methods – means there is little or no need to eliminate waste, unevenness, and unreasonableness. The existence of waste, unevenness, and unreasonableness is beneficial in terms of higher prices; it is a desirable feature of classical management, not a flaw. It standardizes, legitimizes, and normalizes CEOs' use of the Wealth Creation Playbook (see Chapter 1, Table 1-2). In classical management practice, waste, unevenness, and unreasonableness helps business leaders run the business more successfully in a market economy, always in the short-term because of the ever-fluctuating nature of supply and demand. They use the market economy to their advantage. The fact that companies often overproduce (or destroy wealth) does not alter business leaders' underlying logic for ignoring Lean, because overproduction can provide tactical wins in pursuit of larger strategic wins. Thus, there is a large gap between the business logic of money-making and the technical logic of synchronizing supply to demand. Business logic usually prevails.

The purpose of Toyota's production system, boiled down to its most basic essence, is to synchronize supply to demand for competitive buyers' markets. The ability to do so reduces the frequency and severity of stock-out (lost sales) or overproduction of finished goods (resulting in high costs and price discounting). The practical outcome is that production, on average, does not get too far ahead or too far behind actual market demand. Getting it "about right" is good enough. While buyers' markets may set the price, closely synchronizing supply to demand helps the producer maintain close control of pricing (i.e. limit the magnitude of price variation, especially downward prices – loss of profit – due to overproduction). It is preferable for supply to slightly lag demand, but no so much as to keep customers waiting for too long. Tight supplies make the customer feel like they are getting something special, while the producer benefits from steady sales, good prices, and consistent profits.

Despite these benefits, synchronizing supply to demand is not appealing to CEOs, whose attitude can be summed up this way: "It's not my job to synchronize supply to demand. I am always looking to create sellers' markets, to gain leverage, to set higher prices, and increase profit. Lean would interfere with that." The obvious result is that CEOs have no interest in leading a Lean transformation. Any business instinct that might exist to synchronize supply to demand is quickly overrun by profit-seeking behaviors which, in time, become settled habits of thinking and doing.

To the extent that CEOs have any interest in synchronizing supply to demand, that work is left to low-level technicians and the enterprise software system – also known as "the schedule." But, if an opportunity to make money arises, then the schedule is no longer valid. Intervention and imbalance are required, which is where value of waste comes in. Waste is useful because it represents capacity to absorb abrupt changes in output, which will be frequent given business leaders' objective of pecuniary gain. As far as unevenness and unreasonableness, CEOs pay employees to respond when called, whenever they are called. The more practice employees have with unevenness, and unreasonableness, the more skilled they become in managing it. Disruption is a skill to be mastered by employees so that executives can throttle output as-needed.

Fundamentally, classical management operating in a market economy is driven to pursue a profitable price. Toyota management, also operating in a market economy, is driven to pursue satisfying the material wants and needs of the members of society. In classical management, business leaders have virtually no interest in the product, processes, or people; only that the price is profitable. It is the opposite for Toyota management, and presumably true for Lean management as well, recognizing that profits are akin to human nutrition (food energy), whereas loan credit, used liberally in classical management, is akin to steroids (artificially boosting performance) to gain the upper hand.

Finally, it is important to recognize that survival was a primary reason for the creation of the Toyota Production System and The Toyota Way. If management has no interest in the business surviving, meaning it viewed merely as a (private) property that can be sold, merged, or liquidated at any time – whichever is more profitable – then the *raison d'etre* for pursuing Lean management disappears. And since a business is property, executive teams seek to increase enterprise value, and in doing so they choose the simplest means possible: The Wealth Creation Playbook, not Lean.

Lean is an Intangible Asset

For the last 30 years, our eyes have told us this truth: There is a strong consensus of opinion among CEOs that if any of Lean is to be adopted, it is solely its tools. CEOs have expressed little interest in adopting Lean as a comprehensive system of management to replace classical Management. Much of it has to do with a failure to understand the thinking and interests of CEOs – particularly of large publicly-traded corporations, who have long been the main target of interest for Lean transformation.

CEOs think of Lean differently than Lean people do. The latter see it as a necessary way of thinking and working, for the betterment of all. Lean is a needed advancement in leadership and management practice. The former see Lean as an intangible asset, whether in the form of Lean tools or as a management system, that may or may not produce an income or other financial gain attached to the future sale of goods and services, or to the future sale of the company itself. Lean people see Lean as: "How can you not do it?" CEOs see Lean as: "Why should I bother?" These are different questions that expose a huge gap between the thinking of the people who promote Lean management and the thinking of the business leaders who would adopt Lean. The gap has yet to be closed in any significant way despite decades of effort.

Ownership of a company, either directly or by proxy (i.e. the hiring of professional managers compensated via stock options), confers the right to do with the property as one wishes. This includes the right to grow and improve, as well as the right to neglect, abuse, inhibit, or pervert. The rights exercised vary over time and depend primary on the anticipation of financial gain. In other words, if any aspect of Lean is adopted, it is done for the benefit of owners, not for the benefit of employees, customers, suppliers, or the community. Simply put, adopting Lean tools is seen by CEOs as the most efficient way to pursue financial gain, while adopting Lean as a management system is seen as an inefficient way to pursue financial gain – despite evidence that says otherwise. As owners, it is their right to be wrong. It is also their right to neglect, abuse, inhibit, or pervert Lean. And, as owners, they enjoy total immunity when they neglect, abuse, inhibit, or pervert of Lean. They can do what they want to their property.

The end of all business activity is the sale – tangible values – the sale of products and services, or the sale (or purchase) of a business (or parts of a business). The sale, if it is to occur, must be advantageous from a pecuniary perspective. Take the case of selling a business. The owner expects future value in the form of income yielding capacity, which is normally assigned to tangible assets. Intangible assets such as brands, trademarks, or patents, may also permit computation of future income yielding capacity, though the resulting numbers are less accurate owing to various assumptions. However, other intangible assets lack physical substance, such as Lean tools or Lean management, which do not lend themselves to computation of income yielding capacity. Intangible assets that owners do not understand offer no advantage with respect to generating future income. This is why changes in leaders or changes in owners is so detrimental to Lean. A brilliant example of the reversal of a beautiful Lean transformation was the sale of The Wiremold Company (Emiliani et al., 2007).

Some business leaders say, "Employees are our greatest asset." What they should say, to be clear, is "Employees are our greatest intangible asset." Employees are an intangible asset because owners do not know what employees know or the work that they do. Unlike capital equipment purchased to yield a future income, employees are not capitalizable (or depreciable), and so they are not understood by owners as a tangible asset. When someone buys a company, they do not pay for each employee (as property). They pay for employees' knowledge (an intangible asset) and assume responsibility for the payroll. But because owners do not know what employees know, employees have almost no value to the business beyond their financial compensation (wages and benefits). Under such conditions, employees are fired and hired as determined by business exigencies, making it impossible for Lean management to thrive in any form other than the use of its tools.

At best, CEOs view the Lean management system as having possible future value. But because this is probabilistic, Lean must compete against other types of investment that are attractive to owners and which have a much greater probability of yielding future income — income streams that are either known or assumed to be higher than what Lean management can generate. As an intangible asset, what is Lean worth? What is the value of Lean to business owners if it cannot be capitalized? What is a Shingo Prize worth? How do you value it? In the Wiremold example (a 1999 Shingo Prize winner for Excellence in Manufacturing), the value of Lean to the new owner was clearly zero (Emiliani et al., 2007).

A board of directors' view of the worth of a CEO is how skillfully they can manipulate the vast array of tangible assets, as well as selected intangible assets that can be turned into future income streams such as brands, trademarks, and patents. Skillful manipulation of income yielding tangible assets and intangible assets counts for far more than skillful human interaction through enlightened leadership or managerial abilities. This explains why, despite massive expenditures on training and development, corporate leadership functions (and will continue to function) at an amateur level in terms of human relations – but always at a professional level in terms of asset relations.

Reference
Emiliani, B., Stec., D., Grasso, L., and Stodder, J. (2007), *Better Thinking, Better Results: Case Study and Analysis of an Enterprise-Wide Lean Transformation*, The CLBM, LLC, Wethersfield, Conn., pp. 283-290

Problem-Solving and Human Progress

Toyota's management system is built on the true premise, concluded deductively, that problems are integrant to humanity. Because problems diminish human happiness and threaten survival – whether in life or in business – methods must be developed to do two things: solve problems and assure human progress. The principal method used by Toyota is inductive reasoning, as exemplified by the Plan-Do-Check-Act Cycle, where the "Plan" means to formulate a hypothesis that provisionally explains the cause of the problem and then test the hypothesis using the Do-Check-Act portion of the cycle. Problem-solving is, of course, learning.

The truth of a hypothesis, whether well-informed or simply a best-guess, is only probable; it is a plausible, not certain, explanation. If the result of the PDCA cycle is successful (meaning, proved), then the hypothesis infers a general rule. Hypothesis testing is experiential, and so any truth(s) discovered are based on objective facts. But hypotheses can also exist in untested form and be mistakenly understood and used as truth. How does this happen?

A hypothesis can seem to explain the observed data, without formal testing, which will result in sensory satisfaction, emotional contentment, or mental (intellectual) gratification. This form of hypothesis is merely an aesthetic truth, not an objective, fact-based truth, and takes on subjective properties that are close in proximity to the realm of art, beauty, and taste. The seeming validity of aesthetic truths – the "feeling of rightness" – is strongly reinforced by attributing subsets of apparent causal factors to external objects such as folklore, myths, concepts regarded as sacred or time-tested (sentiments), or a deity. Therefore, aesthetic truths are a corruption or contamination of objective, fact-based truths. How are aesthetic truth generated?

Business leaders are often physically located far from where the actual work is performed (or, if near, they rarely visit the workplace). In addition, there is a social distance between top leaders and the employees in lower levels of the hierarchy. There is also a great economic distance (e.g. CEO pay vs. worker pay). These combine to imbue leaders with myriad hypotheses that explain, to their satisfaction, what they think is happening in lower levels of the organization (and among suppliers and customers as well). Their hypotheses exist mostly as aesthetic truths, not as objective fact-based truths. And let's not forget that information provided to leaders is typically suffused with confirmation bias (i.e. telling the leaders what they want to hear), because it is dangerous to tell them objective fact-based truths or to try convincing them that their aesthetic truths are deeply erroneous. One can therefore conclude that, from business leaders' perspective, there is both merit and beauty in waste. Waste is useful – something that can be put into service to produce desired ends.

Importantly, leaders' hypotheses and associated aesthetic truths are socially inheritable – patterns of thinking that are taught by one generation of leaders to the next, resulting in traditions that are very difficult to break or displace. The existence of aesthetic truths and their perpetuation across generations of leaders are important and noteworthy characteristics of classical management.

Toyota's progressive management system possesses three remarkable characteristics, which stand in marked contrast to classical management:

- Concern for people (humanity), welfare of the community, and future well-being (survival)
- Workmanship, with goals of efficiency and avoiding waste
- Curiosity to find and understand the objective truth as informed by facts learned through problem-solving

Concern for people establishes a penultimate purpose and humanizes activities in both life and workmanship, while curiosity – asking "Why?" – challenges preconceptions that threaten human ability to solve problems and helps assure humanity's progress. Curiosity, informed by observation, is actualized systematically through PDCA, kaizen, and other forms or derivatives of the Scientific Method. Their daily use by all employees reduces the chance that individuals or the organization will become dominated or overtaken by mere aesthetic truths with consequent loss of the facts derived from empirical reality.

We know from vast experience that aesthetic truths have from near-zero to zero probability of being in agreement with objective, fact-based truths that have been revealed though careful hypothesis testing. This is perhaps the greatest lesson to be learned from Toyota's work over the last 70 years. It is pleasing to know that some business leaders have cared to recognize the learning and put it into everyday use. Yet, classical management, saturated with aesthetic truths, continues to dominate management practice, assuring that necessary progress does not take place or occurs much slower than is needed by humanity.

The question becomes, simply, which method of management practice is more efficient at solving problems and assuring human progress? Which can deliver more beneficent ends to humanity? A bedrock premise in classical management is that conflict and predation (zero-sum outcomes) are both good and necessary. This premise is obviously at odds with assuring human progress, as it retains obsolete war-like traditions that normalize and routinize regression. A bedrock premise in Toyota management is that cooperation and human welfare (as in health, happiness, prosperity) are both good and necessary. This premise is consonant with assuring human progress, as it continuously seeks to find new methods of achieving beneficent ends.

The requirement for conflict and predation in classical management can be logically argued to be true, yet it is a preconception to think that it is the one best way to solve problems and assure human progress. Toyota (and its predecessor system of progressive management) showed us how to successfully make business an experimental (and evolutionary) science, versus business as a theoretical science (as in classical management due absence or deficiency of experimentation), which has the effect of challenging and destroying preconceptions. That is an amazing accomplishment, but one which continues to languish in relative obscurity.

Six Pictures Tell All

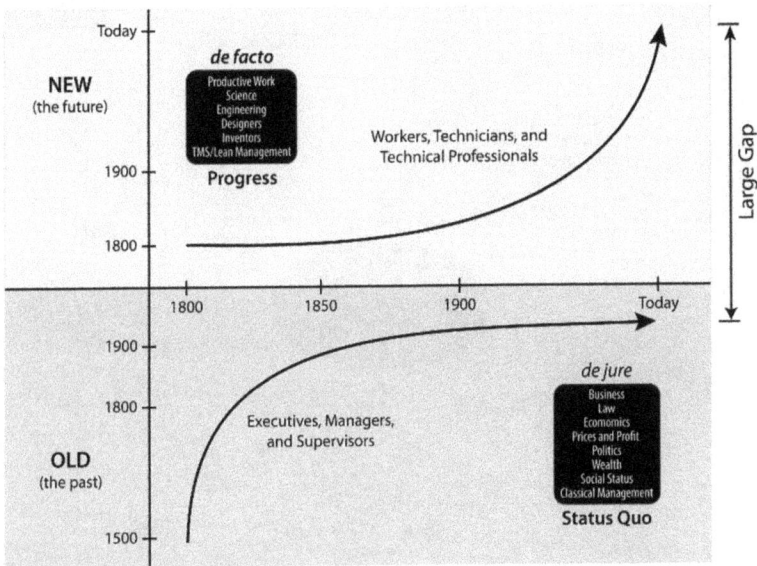

Figure A-3. Lean's dilemma: The ever-present past. The axes depict boundaries (not graph axes) demarking time fields and paths. The large gap (upper right) generates the perception company mismanagement; e.g. incompetence, misalignment, confusion, concealment. "*de facto*" means the thinking and practices based on that which exist in reality: facts, cause-and-effect, logical, scientific method. "*de jure*" means the thinking and practices based on customs, sentiments, prejudices, policies, laws. The population of *de facto* reasoning employees far outnumber the *de jure* leaders. Yet, the few reduce the pace, performance, and product of the many. The cumulative wisdom of tradition prevails because it is more highly valued than logical (scientific) reasoning. Logical reasoning in business is seen as incomplete. Therefore, the ever-present past delays and progress in business and society.

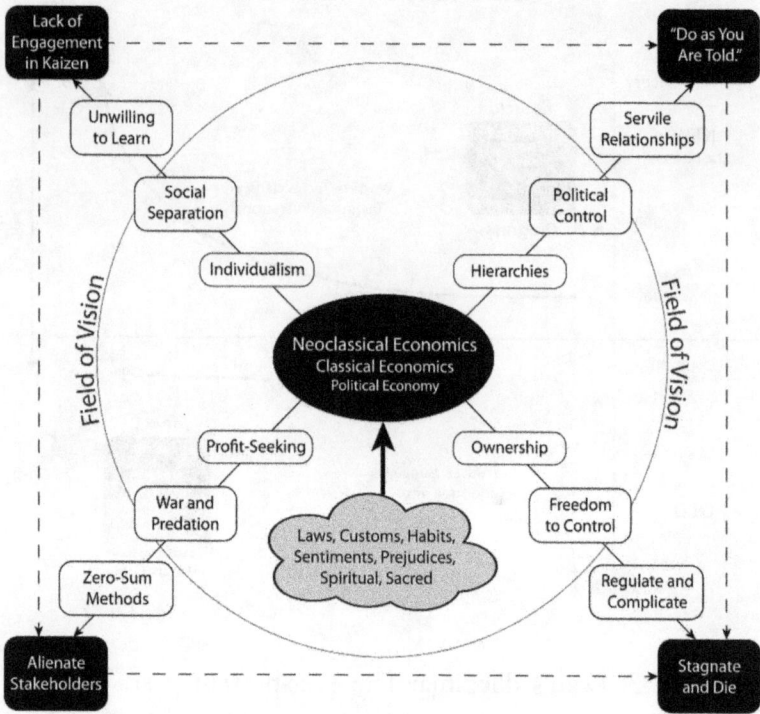

Figure A-4. Network diagram of executive resistance to Lean and Lean transformation failure. It shows the relationships between *de jure* and *de facto* outcomes that result in corporate distress. Corporations are designed for prosperity, not for adversity. Adversity is most often man-made and preventable, as the image shows. When adversity strikes, the usual classical management response is corporate autotomy (self-severing parts of the business to survive; e.g. layoffs, plant closings, squeezing suppliers, and so on).

Figure A-5. Two different houses, two different realities. A stark illustration of the fundamental differences between Toyota's mostly *de facto* management thinking and practice and other businesses' mostly *de jure* management thinking and practice. A quick example illustrates the point: The "price system" (price = cost + profit) thrives, while Taiichi Ohno's "cost system" (price − cost = profit) is of no interest to classical management executives. They find the "cost system," and thus Lean management unappealing. The "price system" has long been institutionalized and executives are habituated to it and other features of classical management.

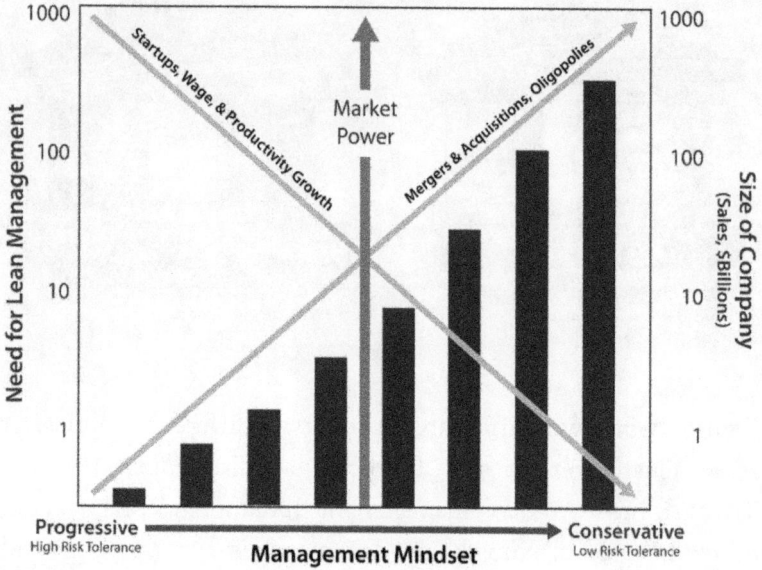

Figure A-6. The LeanX-Diagram. Explains why Lean is not common in large companies and highlights the importance of the realism corner of the business philosophy triangle to classical management executives. Study the image carefully because it tells you a lot about business, the passions and interests of CEOs, and Lean.

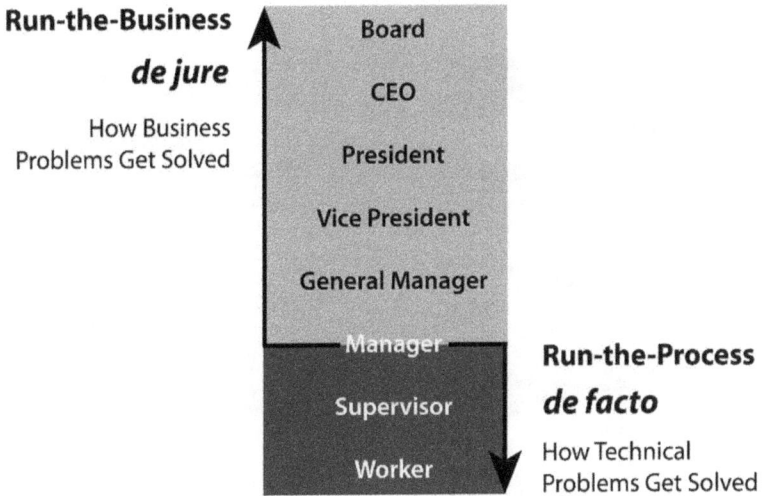

Figure A-7. The business-technical divide. The image illustrates the distinction between *de jure* used for business problem-solving and *de facto* used for technical problem solving. The inflection point comes at the middle manager position. It also explains why executives invariably delegate Lean to lower levels of the organization and technical specialists. The run-the-business versus run-the-process divide is a deeply entrenched preconception that functions as a strong barrier against the uptake of Lean management among executives, whether the corporation is large or small.

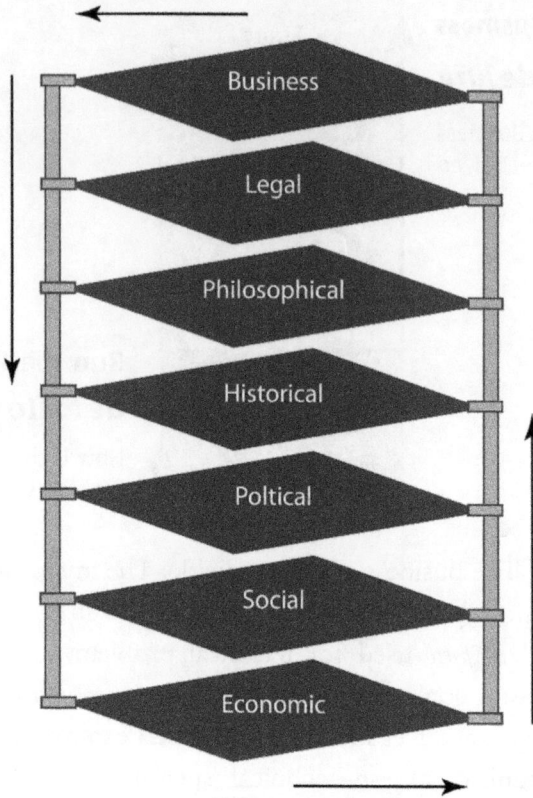

Figure A-8. Stacked cognitive biases. A person is subject to a wide range of cognitive bias (systematic errors in thinking) in any one plane. Executives are subject to cognitive bias in all seven planes. The arrows depict the flow of cognitive biases within a plane and among the planes. This mixing effect generates strong reinforcement of the collected cognitive biases, which makes it very difficult to replace classical management via common means such as persuasion, training, or education.

About the Author

M.L. "Bob" Emiliani is a professor in the School of Engineering, Science, and Technology at Connecticut State University in New Britain, Conn., where he teaches a course on leadership, a unique course that analyzes failures in management decision-making, as well as other courses.

Bob earned a Bachelor of Science degree in mechanical engineering from the University of Miami, a Master of Science degree in chemical engineering from the University of Rhode Island, and a Doctor of Philosophy degree in Engineering from Brown University.

He worked in the consumer products and aerospace industries for 15 years, beginning as a materials engineer. He has held management positions in engineering, manufacturing, and supply chain management at Pratt & Whitney.

Bob joined academia in September 1999. While in academia, he developed the Lean teaching pedagogy and led activities to continuously improve master's degree programs.

Emiliani has authored or co-authored 19 books, four book chapters, and more than 45 peer-reviewed papers. He has received six awards for writing.

Visit www.bobemiliani.com and www.speedleadership.com